handy andy's
HOME WORK

handy andy's
HOME WORK

andy kane

Acknowledgements

I would particularly like to thank Mike Lawrence for his hard work and patience, and also for transforming my typescript into meaningful text; Nicky Copeland, for commissioning the book in the first place; Lisa Pettibone for her creative input; Mark Latter for his innovative design and stylish layouts; Khadija Manjlai for her dedication throughout; Sarah Miles for her thoroughness; and to the rest of the team at BBC Worldwide.

Published by BBC Worldwide Limited,
Woodlands, 80 Wood Lane, London W12 0TT

First published 2000

ISBN 0563 55192 5

Commissioning Editor: **Nicky Copeland**

Project Editor: **Khadija Manjlai**

Copy-editor: **Trish Burgess**

Picture Researcher: **Victoria Hall**

Art Director: **Lisa Pettibone**

Designer: **Mark Latter, Vivid**

Illustrator: **Jason Chapman**

Set in Helvetica
Printed and bound in France by Imprimerie Pollina s.a. - n° L 80208-A
Colour separations by Imprimerie Pollina s.a.

For my wife Geraldine
and for my children
Amy, Ellie and Olivia

contents

getting to know your home

Before you get stuck into some DIY, you need to know what you're up against. This chapter takes you on a quick guided tour of a typical house, helping you to understand how it's been put together and what makes it tick by way of services and fittings.

It also tells you about some of the variations you're likely to find in your own home, whether it's a Victorian terrace or a modern estate house. Knowing what's under the skin of your home will make it much easier to plan and tackle the jobs you want to do, and it will help you avoid many of the commonest DIY foul-ups too. This book starts with a look around the outside of the house, then tackles the main structure – the roof, the walls, floors and ceilings, doors, windows and the stairs. Next it deals with the services – electricity, gas, water (including waste pipes and drains) – plus a typical central heating system. At the end is a section about coping with nasty problems, such as damp and rot, and a guide to help you plan the changes you want to carry out.

the outside view

You can learn a lot about your home just by stepping out of your front door and giving the building a long, hard look. Start at the top and work your way down. If there are parts you can't see easily, either go next door to get a better view, or look at similar houses along the road. Here are some of the features you're likely to see.

UP ON THE ROOF

Assuming you've got a pitched (sloping) roof rather than a flat one, the first thing you'll notice is what's covering it. You'll probably have tiles of one sort or another, unless your house was built before about 1900, when slates were the norm. Both tiles and slates are fixed to horizontal strips of wood called battens, which are themselves nailed across the downward-sloping roof timbers – the rafters. The top of the roof, called the ridge, is finished with shaped ridge tiles which are usually semi-circular and cover the join between the two sides of the roof. Any external angles (hips) between two roof slopes are also topped with ridge tiles. Where roof slopes meet at an internal angle – a valley – there's usually a lead-lined gutter running from top to bottom to carry rainwater away. If your roof has only two slopes, the end walls of the house will be built up into a triangular shape called a gable.

The roof meets the walls at the eaves, which usually project a little beyond the wall face. The ends of the rafters are cut square here, and planks of wood are nailed to them to close off the eaves. The vertical plank is the fascia, and the horizontal one the soffit. Your gutters will be supported on brackets screwed to the fascia. On a modern house, look for ventilators in the soffit: they help to ventilate the loft space. You won't be able to inspect a flat roof from the ground, and there's not much to see anyway. The horizontal roof timbers are covered with boards and then a waterproof layer of either roofing felt or asphalt – a sort of smooth tar. Neither lasts nearly as long as a good tiled or slated roof.

top **The 1930s semi has several standard features, including the two-storey bay windows and a recessed porch.**
above **A typical Georgian townhouse will feature sliding sash windows, some decorative rendering to the ground floor, a front door above street level and probably a sub-basement.**

If you have chimney stacks, use binoculars to take a close look at how they're built. The pot itself sits over the open flue and is held on by a sloping bed of mortar called flaunching. The other important bit is what seals the join between the stack and the roof – usually cut-to-shape lead strips called flashings, but sometimes just a strip of cement mortar.

DOWN THE WALLS

Your house walls tell you a lot about how they're built, especially if they're of plain brickwork. If all you can see are the long sides of the bricks, then you have cavity walls – two separate walls, each one brick thick, set about 50 mm (2 in) apart and held together by metal straps called wall ties. The gap in the middle stops any rainwater that gets through the outer wall from reaching the inner one, and in modern houses it often contains some insulation too.

Cavity walls became common after the First World War. To start with, both walls were built of brick, but it soon became common practice to use insulating blocks for the inner wall. You'll find out what you've got the first time you drill a hole indoors: red drill dust means bricks, grey dust means blocks.

Before about 1920, most houses had solid brick walls, and you can tell if you have these by looking for a pattern of long brick sides and smaller brick ends. You can also tell by measuring the wall thickness at a window opening. It will be about 250 mm (10 in) thick (including the plaster) if it's solid, and 300 mm (12 in) or more if it's a cavity wall.

Of course you might not be able to see any bricks at all because your house has been rendered, pebble-dashed, or covered in timber cladding or hanging tiles. Rendering and pebble-dashing involve coating the brickwork with a layer of cement mortar, either left smooth (rendered), or finished with a layer of fine pebbles pressed into mortar – very popular in the 1920s and 1930s.

above **The Victorian terrace is a feature of every town in the country. Standard features include decorative arches over door and window openings and a tiny front garden.**

There's one last thing to look for near the bottom of your walls – the damp-proof course, known in the trade as the DPC. It's just below indoor floor level, and stops moisture from the ground soaking into the walls and making them damp. In old houses it usually consists of two layers of slates laid between the bricks, while in newer houses, it's a continuous strip of black, waterproof material. You'll be able to see at a glance which you've got…unless your house has been rendered, of course.

walls and partitions

Back indoors, the next part of your home to get the once-over has to be the internal walls. You already know a bit about your outside walls. They're solid masonry, unless you live in a timber-framed house – see the Walls of Wood box, opposite. Now it's time to turn detective on the walls inside – the ones that divide your house into rooms.

SOLID AS A ROCK

The age of your house will give you a good clue as to how your internal walls were built. All the walls on the ground floor will almost certainly be solid masonry because they have to support the weight of the floor above and also the upstairs walls and should never be removed, unless you are preparing other means of support. They're known as load-bearing walls. They'll be built of brick in pre-1920s' houses, and of blockwork in later ones, and they'll be around 130 mm (5 in) thick overall. As with external walls, drilling a hole will reveal which type you have. The surface is finished with a coat of smooth plaster on both sides.

YOU'VE BEEN FRAMED

Some upstairs walls might again be of solid masonry, but only if they're directly over a load-bearing wall downstairs. Otherwise they'll be timber-framed partition walls, acting simply as room dividers. In older houses these walls will be faced with lath-and-plaster – slim wooden battens nailed across the frame timbers and then plastered over – while newer houses will have partitions clad with sheets of plasterboard.

You might find one or two of these partition walls downstairs too, perhaps dividing up large rooms. They'll sound hollow when you tap the wall surface.

TYPES OF EXTERNAL WALLS

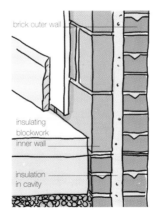

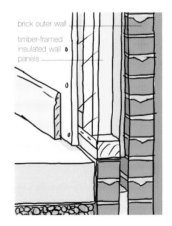

above **Until the early 20th century, exterior walls were of solid masonry – usually one brick (230 mm/9 in) thick and easy to identify from the alternate courses or brick faces and ends visible on the outside of the house walls.**

above **Houses built since about the 1920s have cavity walls – two separate walls with a gap between them. Older cavity walls are all brick, but modern ones have the inner leaf built with lightweight insulating blocks.**

above **Some modern houses have timber-framed inner walls which support the upstairs floors and ceilings. The outer skin of brickwork is a decorative and weatherproof skin which is added when the timber structure is complete.**

TYPES OF INTERNAL WALLS

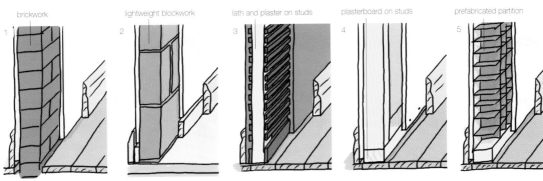

brickwork · lightweight blockwork · lath and plaster on studs · plasterboard on studs · prefabricated partition

above **Interior loadbearing walls may be built in brickwork (1) or lightweight blockwork (2) with a skim coat of plaster on top. Non-loadbearing partitions may be timber frames clad with lath** and plaster (3) in older houses, or with plasterboard (4) in those built since the 1950s. Recently built houses may have partition walls built with prefabricated panels (5).

THE PLASTER TEST

While checking out your walls, there's a simple test you can do to find out what sort of plaster you have on solid walls. Just push in a bradawl or a small screwdriver until it meets some resistance, then pull it out again so you can see how thick the plaster is. Modern houses have relatively hard gypsum plaster that's usually about 13 mm (½ in) thick, while older houses have much softer lime plaster that can be up to 25 mm (1 in) thick.

The plaster thickness is important when you are fixing things to walls (see p108–117) because the screws have to be long enough to penetrate solid masonry.

BRIDGING THE GAPS

Walls have openings in them for doors and windows, and something has to bridge the gap and support the weight of the wall above the opening. That's the job of lintels. They rest on the masonry at each side of the opening, and the wall above them is built up once they're in place. Old houses often have a stout timber beam (plus a brick or stone arch for appearances on outside walls), while newer houses have concrete or steel lintels. You'll find out which you have when you try to drill holes above your windows in order to fix curtain tracks (see page 116).

walls of wood

Timber-framed houses, relatively uncommon in Britain, look just like those built with cavity walls, but apart from keeping the rain out, the outer walls are purely decorative. What holds the house up are the inner walls, which are sturdy timber-framed panels covered with plywood and waterproof building paper on the cavity side, and with plasterboard containing a polythene vapour barrier on the indoor side. The panels are filled with insulation to keep the heat in. You can tell if your house is timber-framed simply by knocking on the indoor surface of the outside walls. Solid walls sound solid, while timber-framed ones sound hollow. You need to know this if you're planning to attach things to these walls (see pages 108–117).

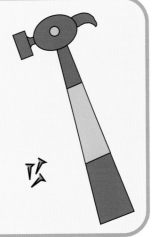

floors and ceilings

Now let's have a look at the surfaces that top and tail each room – the floor and the ceiling. One gets a lot of wear and tear, the other next to none, yet it still pays to know how they've been put together so that you can decorate them appropriately, attach things to them successfully and sort out any faults they develop as time goes by.

GROUND LEVEL

The ground floor of your house might be a solid concrete slab – almost universal in houses built since about 1950 – or might be a suspended timber floor with an air space underneath it if built before then. You can tell which you've got simply by stamping your feet. Solid or direct-to-earth floors are actually a concrete

sandwich – a layer of coarse concrete laid on the ground beneath the house, covered with a plastic sheet – known as the damp-proof membrane or DPM – to keep the floor dry, and topped off with a fine concrete layer called a screed which forms the floor surface proper.

Suspended timber floors have wooden beams called

TYPES OF FLOORS

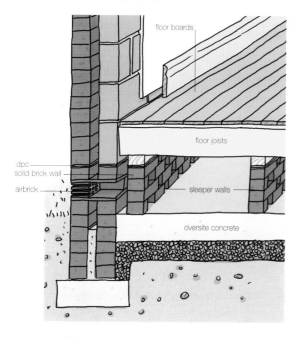

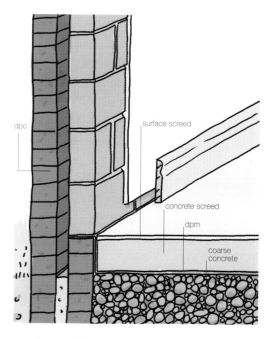

above **Until the 1950s, most houses had suspended timber ground floors, with joists supported on low 'sleeper' walls built up on the oversite concrete. A damp-proof course (DPC) in the walls keeps rising damp at bay.**

above **Houses built since the 1950s invariably have solid concrete ground floors incorporating a damp-proof membrane (DPM) linked to the DPC in the house walls and finished off with a surface screed of fine concrete.**

joists spanning from wall to wall, and are covered with floorboards nailed to the joists. These boards are often square-edged (and very draughty) in old houses. In modern buildings they are more commonly tongued-and-grooved so that they interlock with each other. (In the most modern houses – built in the last ten years – chipboard is used instead of floor boards.) The air space beneath timber floors is ventilated by airbricks low down in the outside walls of the house. This ventilation is essential to keep the timber dry and stop rot from attacking it. Make sure your airbricks aren't blocked up with cobwebs and rubbish.

Newish houses built on sloping sites usually have what appears to be a solid concrete floor, but it is in fact suspended like a timber floor. Special T-shaped reinforced concrete beams span the floor void, with the crossbar of the T facing down. Insulating blocks are laid between the beams, resting on the crossbars, and then a thin concrete screed is laid on top. The result? A floor that's suspended but feels just as firm as solid concrete.

GOING UP

Unless you live in a block of flats, your upper floor (or floors) will be just like a suspended timber ground floor. The joists are supported by the external walls and by internal load-bearing ones, with floorboards or sheets of flooring-grade chipboard laid on top as the floor surface, and lath and plaster (in old houses) or plasterboard on the underside forming the ceiling in the room below. Top-floor rooms are spanned by the roof joists, and have just a ceiling fixed to them unless the loft space above has been boarded over for storage.

CEILINGS

Your ceilings will be made by fixing sheets of plasterboard to the undersides of the ceiling joists if the house was built since about 1950. Older houses will have lath and plaster ceilings: a look in the loft will tell you which type you have.

in the void

The space beneath a timber ground floor, and the gap between ceiling and floor surface in other floors, is the ideal place for housebuilders to hide plumbing and heating pipes and electricity cables. Remember this when you're driving screws or nails into ceilings or floors; hit either, and you could be in big trouble.

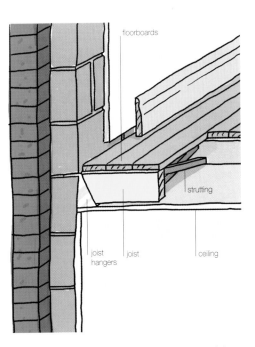

floorboards
strutting
joist hangers
joist
ceiling

above **Upstairs floors are supported by deep timber joists carried on steel joist hangers that are set into the mortar joints in the house wall. Older houses will have floorboards, while more recent ones are likely to have sheets of chipboard instead. Strutting between the joists, often found in older properties, stops the joists from warping.**

doors and windows

Doors don't just let you into and out of the house, or the rooms inside it. Outside doors keep the weather (and burglars) out and the heat in, while inner doors are an integral part of each room's décor. Windows come in all shapes and sizes, in wood, metal and plastic, and may have single or double glazing. Here's how they fit into the building.

DOORS TO THE OUTSIDE

Your front door – and the back door too, if you have one – will be hung on two or three strong hinges within a sturdy timber frame that's fixed to the masonry at each side of the opening. It will probably be a solid timber door, although you might have an aluminium and plastic (uPVC) one if your house has undergone treatment by a replacement window company in the past.

The door frame has a sill which projects beyond the door threshold and slopes down to shed any rainwater

DOOR OPENINGS

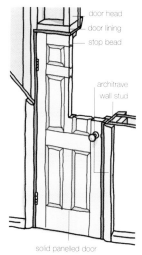

door head
door lining
stop bead
architrave
wall stud

solid panelled door

lintel
door frame
stop bead
architrave

hollow flush door

above **Doors in timber-framed partition walls fit into openings in the framework. A stop bead forms a rebate for the door to close against.**

above **In masonry walls, a lintel bridges the opening and a timber frame lines it. Architrave mouldings conceal the join between frame and masonry.**

that's driven against the door. The frame will probably be nailed to wooden plugs in older homes, or secured with screws and wallplugs in newer ones. Outside doors should be at least 45 mm (1¾ in) thick, so that they aren't weakened by having locks set into their edges. You might have other doors leading to the garden. Outward-opening pairs of glazed timber French windows are a common feature of 1930s' semis, and are making a definite comeback as people tire of patio doors. These are a mixture of fixed and sliding glazed frames fitted into U-shaped door track that's attached to a main door frame. They can be made of wood, aluminium or uPVC, and are almost certain to be double-glazed.

DOORS INDOORS

Internal doors are much lighter-duty affairs – normally only about 35 mm (1¾ in) thick. They can be panelled or flush. Panelled doors might have solid or glass panels, while flush doors might be surfaced with a decorative wood veneer designed to be on show, or with plain plywood or hardboard intended for painting. The hollow interior of a flush door is often filled with a cardboard honeycomb to make it more rigid. There's also a solid timber lock block at each side of the door in which so you can fit recessed latches or locks.

The opening in the wall is fitted with a slim timber door lining and the door is hung on one frame stile. Wooden mouldings called stop beads are nailed to the sides and head of the lining to form a sub-frame against which the door closes.

WINDOW OPENINGS

closing cavities

If your house has cavity walls, the gap has to be closed at door and window openings so that the door or window frames can be fixed in place. This is usually done by placing bricks in older houses or blocks in more recent ones at right angles to the walls, and then plastering over the masonry to form a square-sided opening for the frame. In recently built houses there might be a purpose-made plastic or metal strip rather than solid masonry beneath the plaster.

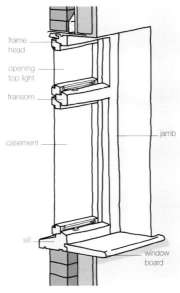

above **Casement windows consist of a frame containing fixed panes and opening casements and top lights.**

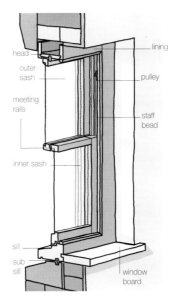

above **Sliding sash windows are supported by weights attached to cords that run over pulleys set in the sides of the frame.**

TYPES OF WINDOWS

Unlike doors with their separate frames, windows come from the factory fully assembled and are usually fixed straight to the masonry at each side of the window opening. Casement windows (those with hinged opening sections) are usually inset slightly from the face of the wall with their sills projecting beyond it. Sash windows, with their vertical sliding panes (the sashes), are set further back and often rest on a stone or tiled sill. The opening is wider on the inside of the wall to create space at each side of the frame for the boxes in which the sash weights are fitted.

Casement windows have a main outer frame, often divided up into separate sections by vertical dividers. Some sections have fixed glass, others have glazed sub-frames that are hinged to the sides of the main frame so that they can be opened. Cross-members fitted near the top of some sections allow smaller top-hung opening frames to be fitted – useful for ventilation when you don't want a main section open. Timber windows – both softwood and hardwood – are by far the commonest, but your home

might have frames in galvanized steel, aluminium or uPVC.

Traditional sash windows are made of timber, which might be further subdivided into small panes, although you might have modern replacements in uPVC with spiral springs instead of weights to hold the sliding sashes in position.

getting to know your home

stairs

Unless you live in a bungalow, you'll have stairs. They might just go straight up in one flight from floor to floor, or perhaps turn corners as they rise – it all depends on the layout of your house. Whatever you have, your stairs are a complicated bit of woodwork, so knowing how everything fits together will make it easier for you to fix any faults in the future.

TYPES OF STAIRS

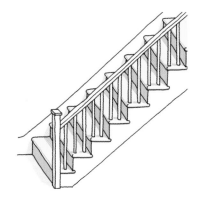

above **An open-string staircase has the outer string cut into steps, with the outer ends of the treads resting on them.**

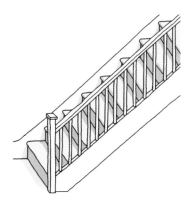

above **A closed-string staircase has side supports (strings) with parallel sides. The treads fit in slots cut into their inner faces.**

THE BASIC INGREDIENTS

Stairs are rather like a ladder, with the treads fitting between two parallel side supports called strings. The ends of treads – and the vertical bits called risers that are fixed between them (unless you have an open-plan staircase) – usually fit into slots machined into the inner faces of the strings, and are held there by wooden wedges. This is a closed-string staircase. It's usually set against a wall, and sometimes there's a wall at both sides if the stairwell is completely enclosed. In this case the two strings are fixed directly to the side walls.

In many older houses the open side of the staircase is cut away in a zigzag shape, and the outer ends of the treads rest on and project slightly beyond the horizontal parts of the cut-outs instead of in slots. This is an open-string staircase.

HANDY HANDRAILS

Even if your stairs have a wall at each side, they need a handrail for safety. This is usually a wooden moulding, either screwed directly to the wall or held away from it on metal brackets. If one side of the flight is open, there's a stout post at top and bottom called a newel post, which is bolted to the floor joists and fitted with a decorative cap.

The handrail runs parallel to the flight, and the space between it and the top edge of the string is usually filled in with a row of vertical balusters, with two or more horizontal rails or with solid panelling. Balusters either sit in a channel nailed to the top of a closed staircase string, or else fit into notches in the ends of the treads on an open-string staircase. The gaps between balusters or rails must be no more than 100 mm (4 in), to stop small children getting their heads stuck. This is a building rule designed to save you having to call out the fire brigade to set them free.

STAIRCASE LAYOUTS

Your stairs can turn corners in one of two ways. They might have wedge-shaped treads called winders, each turning the direction of the flight by around 30 degrees. This type of flight is more common in older houses, where the staircase was oftern built on site rather than being a factory built unit as is installed in more modern houses. More commonly, the treads will be parallel with each other and there will be a small level area part way up the flight. It's called a quarter landing if it's the same width as the flight, and the upper section of the stairs leads off it at 90 degrees to the lower one. If the flight has to turn through 180 degrees there's a double-width half-landing instead, and the upper flight runs back in the opposite direction to the lower one. On stairs like this, there's an extra newel post at each change of direction, so that the handrail can follow the stairs around the corners.

BELOW STAIRS

The amount of space below your stairs depends on their position and style, but there's usually room for an under-stairs cupboard at least. In this case, you can get at the underside of the flight (or most of it) from inside the cupboard. Sometimes the space is incorporated in the hall, and the underside of the flight is covered with lath and plaster in older homes, or with plasterboard in newer ones. This makes repairs much harder to carry out (see page 156).

below **Many staircases turn a corner as they rise. This flight turns through 180 degrees via a rectangular half-landing, and is called a half-turn or dog-leg flight. A quarter-turn flight turns through 90 degrees via a square quarter-landing.**

insulation and ventilation

Houses need insulation to keep them warm in winter and cool in summer because most of the materials used to build houses aren't very good at keeping heat in (or out). They also need ventilation to keep the house and its occupants in good health, and to banish the menace of condensation. Here's what you're likely to have in and around your house.

UP ALOFT

Unless your loft has been converted, its floor should have a layer of insulation between the joists. This will probably be glass fibre or mineral wool blanket, and you should have at least 150 mm (6 in) of it to keep the heat in. If you have less, make it a priority to put an extra layer over what's there. Do ensure, however, that the blanket is kept clear of the eaves to give the loft some ventilation. Otherwise any warm, moist air from the house that gets past the insulation will form condensation in the cold loft, leading to soggy and useless insulation, stained ceilings and rot in the roof timbers.

Your cold water storage tank (page 24) and the heating system's header tank (page 29) should both have an insulating jacket, and any pipework in the loft should be lagged with insulating bandage or foam plastic insulation to prevent it from freezing up during the winter.

INSIDE THE WALLS

If you have a modern house, the cavity in your cavity walls will have been filled with insulation when the house was built. Older houses with cavity walls might have had insulation pumped or blown into the cavity from outside. If you don't know whether it's been

how houses lose heat

- No or inadequate (less than 150 mm/6 in) loft insulation
- Single-glazed windows
- Lack of draught-proofing round windows and doors
- Lack of insulation materials round water tanks and pipes

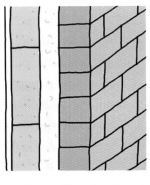

above **Houses with cavity walls may be built with insulation in the cavity, or may have it added at a later date.**

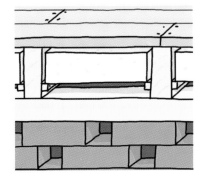

above **Suspended timber ground floors lose heat fast, but you can add insulation beneath them to cut heat losses.**

installed but want to find out, look for signs of patching at regular intervals in the house's outside walls. The patches cover the holes where the insulation was pumped in.

UNDER THE FLOOR

All new homes now have rigid polystyrene foam insulation sheets incorporated into the structure of their ground floors, but few older homes will have any floor insulation. Adding it is out of the question if you have solid floors because you'd end up raising the floor level, but you can fit insulation beneath suspended timber floors if you can be bothered to lift all the boards first. If you can't, go for thick carpets and good underlay instead.

WINDOWS AND DOORS

Window glass is the worst building material of all at keeping heat in, which is why double glazing is now so widespread. You'll know if you've got it, and if you haven't, you could be a candidate for replacement windows, which come with double glazing as standard. If you have single glazing, you could opt to install secondary glazing which is fitted inside the existing frames. It's better than nothing!

Draught-proofing goes a long way towards saving heat losses around doors and windows. Rigid strips with flexible seals are best for doors, while self-adhesive synthetic rubber strips are ideal for windows. If you don't have any draught-proofing, or what you have is in poor condition, fit some now. It's inexpensive, and will pay for itself in a couple of years by cutting your heating bills.

VENTILATION

Kitchens, bathrooms and WCs are the main problem rooms for condensation and lingering smells caused by sub-standard ventilation. Each should have an extractor fan taking steam and stale air straight to the outside air, either through the wall or via ducting in the ceiling above to an external grille. New homes already do; older homes can have one fitted by an electrician and fitting is a relatively easy job. You'll have airbricks fitted in your external walls below floor level if you have a suspended timber floor. These keep air circulating in the space beneath it and stop rot from taking a hold. Make sure they're kept clear of blockages.

In a modern house you will also have small air vents in the soffits (the underside of the eaves) to let air into the loft, and there'll also be slim 'trickle' ventilators at the top of every window frame in houses built since about 1990.

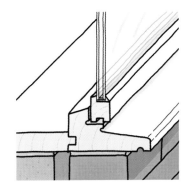

above **Double glazing cuts heat loss through windows and glazed doors by 50 per cent.**

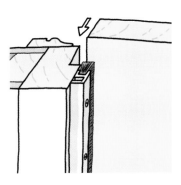

above **Draughtproofing round doors and windows pays for itself in a couple of years.**

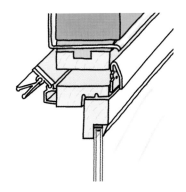

above **Trickle ventilators in the top section of window frames help to prevent condensation.**

electricity and gas

Even if you never plan to do any work on your home's wiring system, you do need to know a bit about how it works. You'll then be able to trace faults when they occur, and fix things without having to go to the expense of calling out an electrician. So let's go and find the start of it all – the fuse box.

a right fuse

There are two main types of fuse used in plugs:
• A 3-amp fuse is suitable for appliances that don't use heat, and a low wattage of less than 700W.
• A 13-amp fuse should be used for appliances with heating elements, such as a toaster or hairdryer.

below **Your electricity supply is protected by a main fuse in the service head. From there, cables run to the meter and on to a modern consumer unit or an old-fashioned fuse box.**

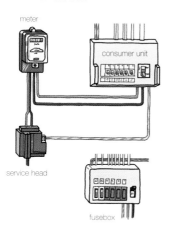

meter

consumer unit

service head

fusebox

THE NERVE CENTRE

Your electricity supply arrives at your house through an underground or overhead cable. It is connected to a sealed unit called the service head. Two thick cables – one red, one black – run from here to your electricity meter, and two more run from there to your fuse box.

Strictly speaking, it's only a fuse box if it contains fuses. Houses built since the mid-1970s – or rewired since then – have what's known as a consumer unit, which contains a row of switches called miniature circuit breakers (MCBs) instead of fuses. They're much safer, and more convenient too. The fuse box or consumer unit acts as a distribution centre, sending electricity through the cables that make up the circuits supplying your lights, socket outlets and major appliances such as cookers and showers.

FUSES AND MCBS

Fuses and MCBs do the same job. They stop the individual circuits in the house from being overloaded. A fuse is a wire that melts when too big a current passes through it, and cuts off the supply to that circuit. If a circuit fuse 'blows', you have to replace it. An MCB detects when the current is too high and simply switches itself off. Once you've reduced the load, you simply switch it back on again.

The fuse box also contains the system's main on-off switch. A consumer unit might also have an on-off switch, or perhaps a residual current device (RCD) acting as the on-off switch instead. This device shuts off the power supply if a current leak develops, or if you receive a shock from touching something live. Since 1992 the main switch has returned, and the RCD now protects only the power circuits, not the lighting circuits, so the lights stay on if the RCD trips off – a valuable safety point.

LIGHT AND POWER CIRCUITS

Light circuit cables run from light to light, and each light's switch cable is usually connected directly into a ceiling rose. With some light fittings, the light and its switch are connected to the circuit cable at a junction box. The circuit is protected by a 5-amp fuse or by a 5 or 6 amp MCB. Power circuit cables run from socket outlet to socket outlet, with both ends of the cable connected into the fuse box or consumer unit so current can flow either way around the circuit: that's why they're usually called ring circuits. Ring circuits are protected by a 30-amp fuse, or by a 30 or 32 amp MCB. Some socket outlets are wired as spurs (branches off the main ring).

You might also have one or two power circuits wired like lighting circuits, with the cable running from outlet to outlet and terminating at the last one. These are called radial circuits, and have either 20-amp or 30/32-amp fuses or MCBs, depending on the floor area they serve.

There may also be individual radial power circuits supplying an electric cooker (45-amp fuse or MCB), an immersion heater (15-amp fuse or 16-amp MCB) or an electric shower (the fuse/MCB rating depends on the shower's power rating).

YOUR GAS SUPPLY

Gas reaches your house through an underground pipe running from the gas main beneath the street. This pipe runs first to the house's main on-off lever, then into the meter and from there via a network of copper pipes (or iron ones in older houses) to supply your boiler, your cooker and anything else that uses gas as its fuel. Each appliance has its own isolating valve. Apart from turning the gas supply on and off, you are not allowed to work on or tamper with any part of your gas system – it's against the Gas Safety Regulations – so don't even think about it.

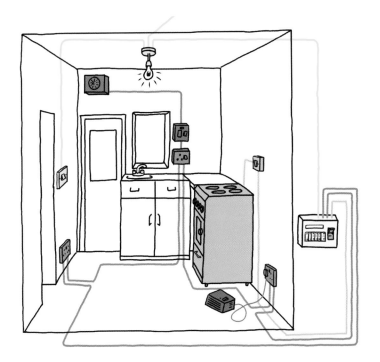

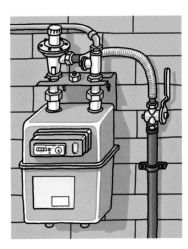

above **Your gas supply runs in via an on-off lever to the gas meter and on to wherever it is needed in the house.**

left **Your home's circuits are all wired from the consumer unit or fuse box. Lighting circuits run out to the most remote light, while circuits supplying socket outlets are wired as rings.**

 lighting circuit spur on a ring circuit ring circuit single-appliance circuit plug-in appliance

water supply

Plumbing systems are like icebergs: all the best bits are hidden out of sight, so finding out what's there can be difficult. Use the descriptions here to identify the bits you can see, and let the diagram do the rest. Then at least you'll know how to cope with a plumbing emergency, even if you never intend to do any actual plumbing work yourself.

THE START OF IT ALL

Your water supply reaches your house through an underground 'service' pipe that's connected to the local water main under the road outside. Somewhere on its run from main to house there will be an isolating valve – usually located at the bottom of a clay pipe and hidden beneath a removable metal cover (often in the pavement outside your property). Find out where yours is, and open it to see if you need a special long-handled key to operate it. If you do, get one from a plumber's merchant and use it to check that the valve will turn easily. Alternatively (and if you can reach) try turning the valve by hand. Call the water board now if you can't shift it. You might need to one day...

INSIDE THE HOUSE

You should have another isolating valve called a stoptap on the supply pipe shortly after it enters the house. This lets you turn off the incoming supply if you have a plumbing leak on the supply pipework inside the house. Find this valve, too, if you don't know where it is, and check regularly that it turns freely.

Just above this stoptap you should find a drain valve, which you can use to empty the supply pipework if disaster strikes. A branch pipe supplies the kitchen cold tap, guaranteeing you a supply of pure water for drinking and cooking. This water will also be a greater pressure than that from other taps in the house, because it's the only one fed directly from the main.

UP TO THE TANK...

Most houses have an indirect plumbing system. The supply pipe, known as the rising main, runs up through the house to the cold water storage tank in the loft or an upstairs cupboard, and fills it via a float-operated valve (ball valve). If you have a conventional heating system, the pipe will also supply a smaller tank – the header tank – which keeps the heating system topped up. Both tanks have overflow pipes, which run from near the top of each tank out to the eaves, so you'll see drips falling if something's wrong.

...AND DOWN AGAIN

Two pipes run from the base of the water-storage tank, and each one should be fitted with an isolating valve. One pipe supplies all the cold taps in the house (apart form the kitchen one), while the other pipe runs to the hot cylinder. Here the water is heated by an electric immersion heater or by a copper heat exchanger linked to the central heating boiler. A pipe runs from the top of the cylinder to supply the hot taps. When you turn one on, the pressure of cold water in the storage tank pushes hot water out of the cylinder to the tap, and this is then replaced by cold water from the tank.

On a new plumbing system you might find isolating valves fitted on the pipe to each tap and WC ball-valve – useful when you have to replace a tap washer or service a WC siphon, as you don't have to drain down pipework. They'll also be on your washing-machine and dishwasher pipes.

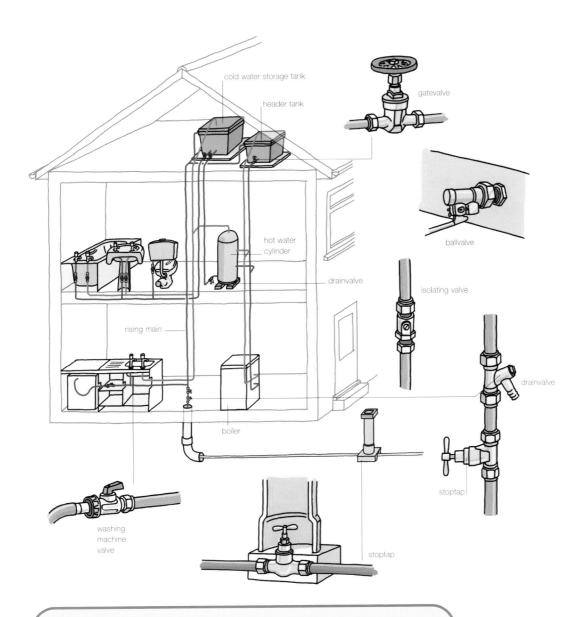

cold water storage tank

header tank

gatevalve

ballvalve

hot water cylinder

drainvalve

isolating valve

rising main

drainvalve

boiler

stoptap

washing machine valve

stoptap

direct systems

In some older houses and in many modern flat conversions, all the water supplied to taps and appliances is at mains pressure. Branch pipes run direct to the cold taps from the supply pipe, and hot water is heated on demand by a boiler or water heater (see page 28) fed by mains-pressure cold water so saving on heating bills. Another advantage of this system is that there are no bulky storage tanks. The main drawback with this system is that you have no stored water available if the main supply is interrupted, and the higher water pressure can also lead to noisy pipework.

waste pipes and drains

Getting rid of the water you use in the home is the job of the waste pipe and drainage system. It has to cope with two types of waste water – the soapy stuff from baths, basins, sinks and washing-machines, and the discharge from WCs. They all end up in the same place – the drains – but they get there in different ways, depending on the age of your house.

SPOT THE PIPES

Older homes usually have a festoon of cast-iron pipework on the outside walls of the house. Waste water from kitchen and bathroom fittings and appliances runs in pipes through the house wall. Pipes downstairs discharge over ground-level gullies – open earthenware pots set in concrete, with a grating to stop leaves and debris blowing into them. Pipes upstairs discharge into open collectors called hoppers, which are fixed to the house wall, and have a bigger pipe, about the same size

coping with rainwater

Rainwater running off the house roof is collected in gutters at eaves level, and then runs into vertical downpipes fixed to the house walls. These usually discharge into gullies, which are linked via underground pipes to surface-water drains beneath the road, or else the water runs into soakaways – rubble-filled pits from where the water seeps away into the subsoil. In some rural areas, rainwater is discharged into the main sewer.

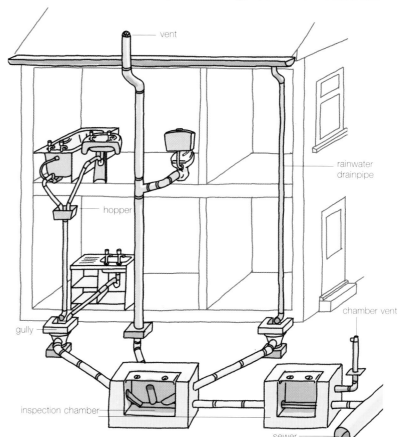

vent

rainwater drainpipe

hopper

chamber vent

gully

inspection chamber

sewer

as a rainwater downpipe, running to a gully below. Each gully then discharges into an earthenware underground drain which runs towards the main sewer. Waste water from the WC runs into a separate 110 mm (4½ in) diameter pipe called the soil pipe. This extends to above eaves level at the top to disperse fumes, and runs down to ground level, where it connects to a separate run of drain pipes.

THE SINGLE-STACK SYSTEM

The gradual introduction of plastic plumbing in the 1960s made the old two-pipe system obsolete. Instead, a single vertical pipe – the soil stack – was designed to take waste water from every appliance, including the WC. To begin with, it was still stuck on the outside wall, but in 1976 new building regulations allowed it to be

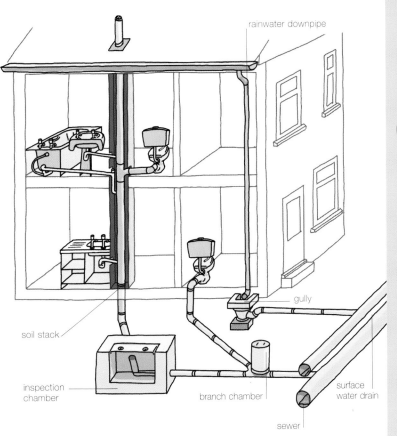

rainwater downpipe

gully

soil stack

inspection chamber

branch chamber

surface water drain

sewer

boxed in somewhere in the house. The result was much neater installations all round, and it became much easier to connect in new pipework as extra fittings and appliances were installed. As increasing numbers of new houses now have more than one bathroom, it's become common for a house to have two or even three soil stacks, and these are now capped off inside the house instead of running right up to roof level.

THE IMPORTANCE OF TRAPS

Underground drains are smelly places, and connecting open pipes to them would let drain smells into the house. That's why every plumbing fitting has a U-shaped section of waste pipe called a trap beneath its plughole. As the fitting empties, the last of the water fills the trap and, if it is deep enough, creates a smell-proof water

seal. If you get a blockage in the trap or the waste pipe, you simply unscrew the trap so that you can clear it. WCs have a trap moulded into the base of the pan, and even gullies have traps. Drain smells have no chance.

WHERE THE DRAINS RUN

The drains running from gullies, soil pipes and soil stacks head first towards one or more inspection chambers (manholes). These are brick chambers or plastic mouldings where the different drains merge. Each has a metal cover, which you can lift to gain access to the drains if any of them becomes blocked. One drain runs from the last inspection chamber and into the main sewer – usually beneath the street outside, but sometimes running across back gardens instead on sloping sites. See pages 122–3 for how to cope with blocked drains.

heating systems

If your old house has never been modernized, you'll still have a fireplace in every room. However, most people now enjoy the benefit of whole-house central heating, and by far the most common system is one where a boiler heats the water and a pump circulates it through a circuit of pipes to a radiator in each room. This is called a wet central heating system because it's hot water that delivers the heat.

THE HEART OF THE SYSTEM

The powerhouse for every central heating system is the boiler. This can be fired by gas (by far the most widely used fuel), oil or solid fuel, and can hang on the wall (gas only), stand on the floor, or even sit in a fireplace recess. The boiler usually heats the house's hot water too. It's controlled by a programmer, which you set to switch the system on and off when you want, and by several thermostats that regulate the way it runs while it's on. It's a good idea to have boilers

serviced to keep them trouble-free. On average, you can expect a boiler to give you up to twenty years, but bear in mind that new models on the market will be more efficient.

PIPES AND PUMPS

A system that heats both rooms and water has two separate pipework circuits. One runs to a heat exchanger inside the hot-water cylinder (see page 25), while the other runs around the house from room to room, carrying

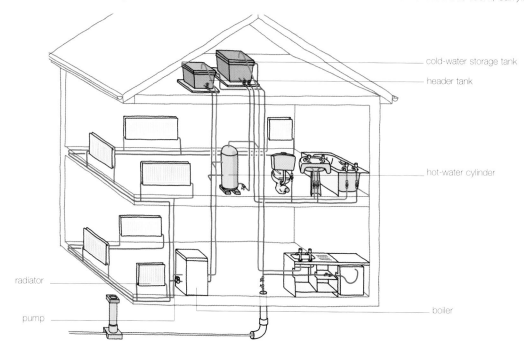

cold-water storage tank

header tank

hot-water cylinder

radiator

boiler

pump

hot water to and from the radiators that heat the air and warm the rooms.

The pipes on the heating circuit are usually 15 mm (½ in) in diameter and known as smallbore pipes, but ones as narrow as 8 or 10 mm (⅜ or ½ in) can be used on a microbore system. They generally run beneath the floorboards, or in ducts in a solid concrete floor, emerging only when they connect to a radiator. The circuit has parallel flow and return pipes running from radiator to radiator, terminating at the last one on the circuit.

Both of these circuits are usually served by a pump which circulates the water around one circuit or the other. The flow is switched between the circuits by a valve, which is activated by the room and cylinder thermostats. If the room thermostat senses a drop in air temperature, it turns the boiler on and opens the valve so that hot water flows round the radiator circuit. If the cylinder thermostat detects that the tank is cold – perhaps because someone has had a hot bath – it does the same to divert heated water to the hot-water circuit.

RADIATORS AND VALVES

Radiators – usually pressed-steel panels, but other types are available such as cast-iron or aluminium – are mounted on the wall and have a valve at each end. One is set by the person who installed the system, to balance the flow rate around the circuit and ensure that the last radiator is just as warm as the first one. The other is either a simple on-off valve, which you turn to control the amount of heat the radiator emits, or else a thermostatic valve, which allows you to set the precise air temperature you want each room to achieve. For how to bleed radiators, see pages 150–1.

TOPPING-UP TIME

Most wet heating systems are open to the atmosphere at a small tank in the loft called the header tank. This tops up any losses from the system, absorbs the expansion of its water as it heats up, and also provides an open-vent

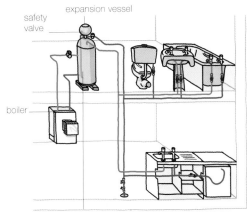

hot-water cylinder

above **Many modern homes have an unvented hot-water system, which does away with the need for a cold-water storage tank in the loft. If the boiler also provides central heating, there will be no feed-and-expansion tank either. The expansion vessel copes with expansion and contraction of the water within the system as it heats and cools.**

pipe to act as a 'safety valve' if the system overheats.

Some of the latest heating systems are closed (sealed) rather than open, so there's no header tank or loft pipework. Instead, expansion is taken care of by a pressure vessel, and there's a special safety valve that lets steam escape if overheating occurs.

electric heating

Some homes have an electric storage heater in each room. These have special heat-absorbing blocks inside, which are heated overnight by cheap-rate electricity, and then give off heat gradually during the day to warm the rooms. Electric underfloor or ceiling panels can also be used to heat rooms, but these have to be installed as the building is constructed. You're more likely to have either of these in a block of flats rather than in a house.

damp, rot and woodworm

Damp is what your house gets if it stops being waterproof. Rot is what the wood in your house does if it gets damp and is then attacked by the same sort of fungus that rots trees in woodland. And woodworm is what happens when wood-boring insects lay their eggs on structural timbers or wooden furniture. Each is bad for your house's health – and often for your pocket too.

below **If the damp-proof course (DPC) in the house walls fails, the most effective way of creating a new DPC is to inject special waterproof chemicals into holes drilled in the walls at the level of the existing DPC. They soak into the masonry and form a permanent water-resistant barrier.**

TWO SORTS OF DAMP

Water gets into your house from the outside in two different ways. The first is upwards from the ground below, either because there's no damp-proof course (DPC) in the house walls, or because the DPC has failed – perhaps because of slight subsidence of the building due to faulty foundations. This is called rising damp. The second, penetrating damp, is the result of a failure in some part of the house structure that ought to be keeping the weather out, but isn't.

Rising damp causes tell-tale damp patches in ground-floor walls, often rising to a height of a metre (3 ft) or more. It can be cured by drilling holes in the affected walls along the level of the existing DPC, and then pumping in special chemicals to form a waterproof layer in the masonry. You can do the job yourself, or call in a professional firm to do it for you.

Penetrating damp usually has a specific cause – a missing roof tile, for example, or rain being blown in around poorly fitting doors or window frames. To cure the problem, all you have to do is find the weak spot and fix whatever is wrong (see pages 128–129). Often this is easy, but sometimes water runs along ceiling joists or down walls, and appears indoors a long way from where it is actually getting in. This is particularly true of flat roofs. Keeping your house in good condition via regular check-ups (see Chapter 5) will go a long way towards avoiding problems such as these.

Damp also has another unwanted side-effect if it's not cured. It causes rot.

SPOT THE ROT

Rot can attack indoors or out. Any exterior woodwork is potentially at risk, but the commonest site for an outbreak is in wooden windows. They have many joints where paint can crack, letting water in and then trapping it under the paint film so that the wood stays damp and rot can spread unnoticed. The wood becomes spongy, and eventually breaks up if it is not treated. This is known as wet rot, and it also attacks garden fences and outbuildings, as well as house woodwork (see pages 150–1 for how to deal with it).

Indoors, both rising and penetrating damp can lead to wet rot in roof and floor timbers, skirting boards and any other affected woodwork. So can plumbing leaks.

But far more dangerous is rot that's caused by another fungus, leading to what is known as dry rot. Here fungus spores develop into a growth called a fruiting body, which spreads more spores and feeds itself via a cobwebby mass of fibres, which can travel through masonry in search of fresh wood to attack. It develops most commonly under suspended timber ground floors, and also behind wooden wall panelling and the lath-and-plaster wall finish often found in old houses. Affected wood splits and cracks into tell-tale cubes, and is effectively dried out by the fungus. Get dry rot, and you've got big trouble. It needs professional treatment to cure it. Companies will usually give you a guarantee, but whether a company is still trading by the end of the guaranteee period will depend on how big and commercial it is.

above **Wet rot will attack any woodwork that becomes damp and exposed to the elements due to failure of its protective paint or varnish coating. Mild outbreaks can be repaired using wood filler after the rotten areas have been removed, but large-scale attacks can only be cured by cutting out the affected wood and replacing it with new wood that has been treated with wood preservative.**

woodworm

Several species of wood-boring flying insects seek out bare wood surfaces in houses on which to lay their eggs. Common sites for an attack are in the loft, under the stairs, on the tops of doors and on the bare backs of wooden furniture. The eggs hatch, and the grubs tunnel their way into the wood to feed. Eventually, they mature into full-grown insects, which eat their way to the surface and leave those tell-tale exit holes. Everyone calls this woodworm, irrespective of which insect did the damage. While the holes can be unsightly, woodworm rarely cause structural damage, and treatment with special chemicals is usually very effective.

small improvements

Hardly anyone has the perfect home – the house where everything is just the way they want it. There's always something that could be improved, whether it's better lighting, increased storage space or a more attractive garden shed. Here are some suggestions for relatively small-scale projects you might be thinking of tackling yourself (or getting a man or two in to do for you). The big home improvements are overleaf.

above **A fitted bedroom not only provides all the built-in storage you could possibly need, it also gives the room a streamlined look and is a positive incentive to keep the place neat and tidy.**

FITTED BEDROOMS

Now that everyone's had a fitted kitchen for years, the unit manufacturers want us all to have fitted bedrooms too. If you sign up for one, you'll get wall-to-wall cupboards, a proper dressing-table, units to fit odd nooks and crannies, lots of clever built-in storage ideas and a clutter-free room that you'll want to show visitors. You'll also probably discover that your bedroom's bigger because everything is much more compact. A good improvement.

BETTER LIGHTING

There's no excuse for lousy lighting, so if you have just a traditional pendant light in the centre of the ceiling and the odd table lamp here and there, get down to your nearest lighting showroom and see what's available. The latest trend is for halogen lighting, which is white and cool and looks stunning. This type of low-voltage lighting is also cheaper to run than lights operating at main voltage because the little bulbs last far longer than ordinary light-bulbs, and many of the sets work off a transformer (a device that reduces the mains voltage of 240 volts to a much lower voltage). This means that the lights use less electricity, which helps to cut down your bill. You can install the fittings yourself if you have sufficient electrical knowledge, otherwise leave the job to an electrician. A brilliant idea!

DOUBLE GLAZING

We're not talking the full Monty of replacement windows here, but the installation of what's called secondary glazing. This involves fitting an extra layer of glass – usually as sliding or hinged panes – inside your existing windows. It's much cheaper than new windows, can be taken down and stored in summer and will also help cut noise pollution if you live on a busy road. And it'll cut your heating bills too. Unsexy but sensible.

A NEW BALUSTRADE

If what lets your staircase down is a really old-fashioned balustrade (that's the handrail plus whatever fills the space beneath it), consider treating yourself to a new one. You can now buy everything you need – end posts, handrail, posh balusters and all the fittings and fixings – in kit form. Available in a variety of woods, the kits can be used by anyone with a bit of woodworking skill. The results are smart and impress visitors.

A FRONT PORCH

A front door that opens straight into the hall means an icy blast right through the ground floor whenever you open the door. You need a porch. If your front door is recessed, you might be able to create an enclosed porch and an outer front door quite easily by using standard window and door frames fitted at the outer edge of the existing covered porch area. If not, you'll have to build a structure that projects from the front of the house – probably a job for the professionals. Either way, a porch is definitely a welcome improvement.

HELPING THE DISABLED

If someone in the family is elderly or disabled, there are lots of things you can buy or create to make life easier and safer. Simply get in touch with your nearest disabled living centre, the Disabled Living Foundation and voluntary bodies such as Arthritis Care, the British Red Cross and the Royal National Institutes for the

above **One of the most popular outdoor improvements is a timber deck to replace an ageing masonry patio. Decks are particularly good at coping with sloping sites, because it's easy to link different levels with steps.**

Blind and for Deaf People which provide literature, advice and products. Thoughtful, and could change someone's life.

OUTDOOR EXTRAS

You can plan all sorts of improvements for the great outdoors, ranging from the latest big thing – a timber deck instead of a patio – to buying a new greenhouse or garden shed, putting up a simple lean-to carport or having a new driveway laid. They're all good added-value improvements – you'll enjoy them the minute they're finished, and they'll boost the house price, too, if you ever sell up and move. Go for it.

big improvements

The improvements on pages 32–3 are the sort of projects you could probably finance out of your savings, or with a modest overdraft. The ones on these pages are more ambitious. They're the sort of large-scale projects that involve borrowing to match – perhaps an extension to your mortgage or a fairly hefty secured bank loan. But they'll be worth it...

above **Adding a conservatory is a favourite way of gaining extra living space at the back or side of the house. If you decide to buy one, don't forget to make provision for winter heating as well as summer ventilation and blinds to keep the sunshine at bay.**

A HOME EXTENSION

If you and your family have run out of room but can't face moving house, a home extension is probably the best answer. Of course, you've got to have the space to build one, but most houses can be extended at the back, even if there's no room at the side. At the end of the day you want your extension to look like part of the original house, so get plenty of professional help with the planning as well as with the building. Done well, this improvement will put serious pounds on your house's value. Done badly, it won't.

A CONSERVATORY

Adding a conservatory was one of the most popular home improvement projects of the 1990s, as replacement window companies began to run out of customers and turned to selling glass buildings instead. A conservatory gives you an extra living room, dining room or children's playroom, and it can be built with minimum disruption to the household. On the down side, it can cost a lot to heat in winter, can get unbearably hot in summer and makes cleaning or decorating upstairs windows a bit tricky. They're great for tropical plant fans, though. Think twice before you decide.

A LOFT CONVERSION

Unless you have a flat roof, using all that vacant space in your loft could be an alternative to building a home extension, especially if you want just extra bedrooms. The loft floor will need strengthening, you'll need dormers or roof windows, and you'll lose some space on the floor below for the staircase, but you'll get the extra rooms you want and spectacular rooftop views into the bargain. Again, get professional help to make the most of the conversion,

especially if you have a modern home with a roof built using trussed rafters: in this case the roof structure will need rebuilding to make space for the rooms. Less added value than an extension, but potentially lots of character.

A NEW KITCHEN

Nothing sells a house like an up-to-date kitchen, and fashions do change with the decades. There are plenty of firms offering complete packages, from design to installation, but if you're happy with the way your kitchen works, why not consider a facelift instead of a whole new installation? New doors and drawer fronts for your existing units, plus new worktops, sink and appliances, could give you an as-new kitchen for a lot less than you might expect. Think about it.

REPLACEMENT WINDOWS

If you need replacement windows, fine...but don't automatically think uPVC. Their thick frame sections don't suit every house, and you shouldn't discount matching what you have with high-performance hardwood windows instead. They'll last a lifetime, and they need next to no maintenance thanks to the durability of high-performance wood stains. They're double-glazed, draught-stripped and offer excellent security, too, but the choice is yours...

above **A fitted kitchen is still every cook's favourite dream. The latest trend is towards light colours and simple uncluttered designs.**

above **Select replacement windows with care to make sure they match the style of the house. The wrong type can really spoil its looks.**

A NEW BATHROOM

Bathrooms are being viewed increasingly as somewhere to escape and relax after a hard day's work, and luxury is definitely the watchword. Replacing your old bathroom suite with a modern combined bath and shower enclosure means you can choose how to bathe without wasting valuable floor space on a separate shower cubicle. This could then let you squeeze in his-and-hers washbasins, or the bidet you've always wanted. You could even consider moving the whole caboodle to a spare bedroom, and really going to town with a big second bathroom fit for a film star. Why not?

CENTRAL HEATING

If you haven't got it, central heating is a must-have home improvement, both for your present comfort and your

above **A well-planned and attractively decorated bathroom is the perfect place to relax at the end of a hard day's work. Make sure you provide plenty of storage for toiletries, and add a plant or too for a natural touch.**

future prosperity: some house-buyers will not consider a house with no heating. Go for a high-efficiency boiler, running a closed system (see pages 28–29) with all the relevant safety devices, and ask your plumber to use plastic pipework rather than copper. Plastic, now fully approved for use, is flexible enough to be installed with far fewer joints than traditional copper, and less prone to plumbing noises and pinhole leaks. Give the system a really modern look with the very latest in radiator designs.

A HOME OFFICE

As more and more people now work from home either part-time or full-time, finding space in the house for an office is a growing priority. If you have a spare room to use, fine. If not, consider converting the garage, adding a small single-storey extension or even building a log cabin in the garden. Remember that you'll need light, power and telecom connections to cope with the IT revolution. A seriously up-to-date improvement idea.

A BASEMENT CONVERSION

If you have a basement, don't waste it on storing junk or growing mushrooms. The space could make a fabulous games room, a perfect hideaway for teenagers or a state-of-the-art home entertainment suite with cinema, surround-sound hi-fi and all the computer games you could want. So long as the rooms are damp-proofed and properly heated and ventilated, the possibilities are endless. Plus points: it's there already, and because it's below ground you won't annoy the neighbours with any noise from it.

A SWIMMING POOL

If you want a pool, make it in-ground and indoors – in other words, in a purpose-built enclosure rather than out in the open. This will let you make full use of what is an expensive luxury. Although it might mean almost breaking the bank, a swimming pool will not add enormously to the value of your house.

rules and regulations

Lots of home improvements need official approval, or have to comply with regulations. The main rules are laid down in the Town & Country Planning Acts, Building Regulations, your water company's bye-laws, the Wiring Regulations and the Gas Safety Regulations. Here's how they affect popular DIY projects.

INTERNAL ALTERATIONS

You're likely to need Building Regulations approval from your local authority if you plan to:
- convert a loft
- alter the positions of bathroom fittings, create a separate WC or put a basin or shower in a bedroom
- create a through room from two smaller ones
- partition a larger room to make two smaller ones
- make a new door or window opening
- convert a garage into living space
- put in new heating appliances

EXTERNAL ALTERATIONS

Local controls can restrict what you want to do. Apply to your local authority for planning permission if you want to:
- build a home extension (Planning permission may not be needed, but always check with your local authority first. You'll also need Building Regulations approval.)
- add a conservatory (but exempt from Building Regulations control if under 30 sq m (324 sq ft) in area)
- build a porch (but exempt from both planning and building control if below a certain size)
- put up a garage or carport (if within 5 m (15 ft) of the house; usually exempt from Building Regulations control)
- create a new entrance to your property from the road (You'll need consent from your local authority highways department to cross a public footpath or verge.)
- put up large outbuildings
- erect fences or walls over 1 m (3 ft) in height next to the road, or over 2 m (6 ft) elsewhere.

You might also have to comply with local authority bye-laws, any restrictive covenants applying to your property, and the strictest rules of all if you live in a listed building or are in a conservation area or an area of outstanding national beauty. As with Building Regulations approval, ask your local authority before going ahead with the job.

WATER, ELECTRICITY AND GAS

You must give your water supply company at least five days' notice if you plan to install a new bidet, WC and cistern, outside tap or swimming pool. In Scotland, you must inform them if you plan to alter/install any water fitting.

Electrical work should meet the requirements of the Wiring Regulations (and must do so in Scotland where they have the force of law). For safety's sake, don't do anything unless you're competent and know exactly what you're doing; leave it to a qualified electrician – either a member of the Electrical Contractors Association (ECA) or someone who is on the roll of the National Inspection Council for Electrical Installation Contracting (NICEIC).

Don't even think of working on your gas supply system or equipment. It's illegal and dangerous. Employ someone who's registered with CORGI (Council for Registered Gas Installers) or who works for your gas supply company.

buying for diy

Kitting yourself out can be expensive unless you know what you need and where to get it. This chapter tells you about paint, wallcoverings, tiles, flooring and wood, recommends what hand and power tools to buy and tells you what is and isn't essential.

You'll probably do most of your shopping at one of the big sheds, as the DIY superstores are called, but don't stick to the same store all the time. Visit local branches of other chains to check out different brands and special offers.

DIY sheds don't carry flooring on a roll, so find a local carpet warehouse, where you can see carpet, sheet vinyl and the 1990s' comeback kid, linoleum, all on display in sample books and on the roll, ready to take away. The worst price deal at the sheds is on wood. Both ordinary softwood – usually pine – and man-made boards, such as MDF (medium-density fibreboard, the DIY woodworker's favourite sheet material), are expensive. If you use a lot, find a local timber merchant. They know wood inside out, and they'll cut stuff to size so you can get it in your car. They'll also save you a lot of money.

paints, varnishes and stains

We use more paint than any other DIY product, which is why such a huge variety is available. The trouble is, this choice can be very confusing when you're standing in the store trying to decide which product to buy. This guide to what's what will make it easier for you to find exactly what you want for each job.

EMULSION AND GLOSS

You'll need just two different paints for most of your home decorating. Number one is emulsion paint, which goes on walls and ceilings and comes in a huge range of colours. It's water-based, so cleaning your painting equipment is quick and easy. It also dries fast – you can apply a second coat if you need to after only three or four hours. Emulsion comes in matt and satin or silk (semi-gloss) finishes, and most people choose the non-drip type because it's easier to handle than the runny but cheaper variety used by professional decorators. Number two is gloss paint, which is used on wood and metal indoors and outside and dries to a shiny gloss finish. Available in hundreds of colours, its main drawback is that it's solvent-based, so it takes longer to dry than emulsion paint and can't be given a second coat until the next day. Until completely dry, it also has a smell that lots of people really hate. Another drawback is that gloss needs a primer and an undercoat – special paints that seal and colour the surface ready for the top gloss coat – if you're painting bare wood or metal. You can buy runny and non-drip varieties. If you want a softer finish than the high gloss, look out for satin gloss and eggshell paints.

aerosol paints

paint for metal

sample pots

gloss paint

emulsion paint

paint terms

Acrylic or vinyl emulsion? Alkyd gloss paint? Polyurethane varnish? What do they all mean? They're simply terms that describe the sort of man-made chemicals used in modern paints to bind the pigment (colour) particles together as the paint dries.

OTHER TYPES

There are lots of other paints on the market, mostly designed to do exactly what it says on the tin – blackboard paint, radiator enamel, masonry paint, garage floor paint and the like – so selecting the one you need is quite simple. But there are a couple you might want to try for more general decorating.

Microporous paints are for new outdoor woodwork. Unlike gloss paint, they're porous, which means they keep rainwater out, but allow any moisture that gets under the paint film to escape through it as water vapour. That means they don't blister and crack as gloss paint does, so they last longer and don't need much maintenance – you just wash them down and put another coat on when the old paint begins to look a bit scruffy. However, they don't work over existing gloss paint, so don't waste time and money using them there.

Textured paint is a thick emulsion that can be used on ceilings (and walls if you want to) to create a three-dimensional surface effect. They are applied thickly with a brush or roller, then given a surface texture with special tools such as combs, embossed rollers and the like.

TESTING TESTING

You can buy tiny tester pots of emulsion, gloss and masonry paints in order to try out various colours before making your mind up. Buy a roll of lining paper (page 42), cut off decent lengths and paint them in your sample colours. Tape or hold them to the surface you'll be decorating to judge the effect: less messy than painting little squares of different colours all over the house.

VARNISHES AND STAINS

If you like to see wood grain on show, you want a clear varnish – basically paint with no colour in it. Water-based acrylic varnish is quick-drying, easy to clean from brushes and hard-wearing. It can be used on wood floors too. If you want a finish that's really tough – on a front door, for example – choose a solvent-based polyurethane varnish instead. Use it straight after breakfast, though, or you won't be able to close the door that night without it sticking fast! You can also buy varnishes with a hint of colour, either wood shades, such as oak and mahogany, or brighter colours, such as red, yellow, green, blue and so on. They give the wood a subtle colouring because they are just a surface coating. If you want deep, strong colours, use a wood dye instead. This penetrates the wood, changing its colour dramatically. You can then use a clear varnish over the top to protect the surface.

textured emulsion paint

top tip

Store paint pots upside down to prevent a skin forming.

coloured varnishes   exterior woodstain

wood dye

wall coverings and tiles

Paint isn't the only thing you can put on walls and ceilings. There's a massive range of wall coverings and tiles you can choose from to give pattern and design, as well as colour. Most wall coverings are paper-based, but you can also get paper-backed fabrics which can look really luxurious. Most tiles for walls are ceramic, but there are also metallic and cork tiles on the market.

TAKING THE STAIN

Ordinary wallpaper is simply paper with a design printed on it. That means it's fairly fragile, and it will also mark and stain easily, so don't use it in areas that might get splashed or touched by sticky little fingers. If this is likely, go for a washable paper – printed paper with a clear plastic surface coating – or an even tougher vinyl wallpaper. This has two layers. The design is printed on the top plastic layer, which is stuck to a paper backing so you can hang it just like ordinary paper. Once it's up, you can actually scrub the surface so long as you take care near seams and edges, making it the perfect wallcovering for messy or steamy rooms such as kitchens, bathrooms and kids' bedrooms.

PLAIN OR FANCY

You can have texture instead of pattern if you want, by choosing one of the so-called relief wallpapers. Some, such as Anaglypta, are embossed in random or regular patterns, but because the relief is hollow, it can be flattened by careless hanging or surface wear. Woodchip wallpaper is a thick, pulpy paper with chips of wood embedded in it. When up, it makes your walls look like they've been coated in thick porridge, but it's cheap, quite tough and a great cover-up for poor plaster with an uneven surface. If you want crisp surface detail and top wear resistance, go for Lincrusta. This is a traditional wall covering made by bonding a solid layer of linseed oil and fillers to a paper backing and then embossing a design on it. It comes in rolls or as flat panels, and is ideal for use below a dado rail – the part of any wall that gets the

machine-made tiles

most knocks and scuffs. These three wallpapers are meant to be painted over, so you can change your colour scheme easily without having to strip the walls first. This makes them about as durable as a washable paper in terms of stain resistance, but most marks wash off them fairly easily.

POSH PAPER

Apart from exclusive hand-printed wallpapers, the most expensive wall coverings around are flocks and fabrics. Flock papers, often seen in Indian restaurants, have designs that incorporate a raised surface pile made by sticking short fibres to the paper backing. Traditional flocks are rather fragile, but modern vinyl flocks are as tough as any other vinyl.

Fabric wall coverings are made by sticking plain or patterned materials such as hessian, silk, suede, wool strands and the like, to a paper backing.

They look great in small areas, but are generally too expensive for wider use, and they need very careful hanging to avoid marking the surface. One for the professionals, I think.

TILES FOR WALLS

Ceramic wall tiles are probably the toughest wall covering you can have in the home. Once they're up and grouted, they'll resist water, steam, surface wear and just about any stain, but the grout can become discoloured as time goes by; use bleach to retouch small areas of grout. Tiles come in a massive array of colours and designs, in sizes ranging from tiny mosaic pieces to slabs as big as 300 mm (12 in) across. Squares and rectangles are the most common shapes, but you can also get interesting interlocking tiles too. They're usually about 4 mm (just over ⅛ in) thick, but some hand-made tiles are a bit thicker. They're all sold in boxes; the number you get depends on the tile size, but 25s and 50s are the most common. Check before you buy.

Wall tiles used to have glazed edges, and some still have two adjacent edges glazed so that they can be left exposed when you're tiling just part of a wall. But these days it's neater to finish off the edges either with a plastic trim, or with a row of ceramic border tiles.

Metallic tiles aren't widely available, but if you can find them, they make an unusual feature – either used on their own or mingled with ceramics. Cork tiles make a cheap and cheerful notice-board, but they seem to have fallen out of favour as a wall covering for larger areas.

what's on a roll?

Nearly all wall coverings come in rolls 520 mm (20½ in) wide and 10.05 m (33 ft) long. There's a handy chart on page 63 to help you estimate how many rolls you'll need for walls and ceilings. Posh papers are usually sold by the metre (just over 3 ft) from rolls that come in a variety of widths.

hand-made tiles

floor coverings and tiles

There is even more product choice when it comes to covering floors. Most people pick carpet for living areas, and go for something more practical, such as sheet vinyl or floor tiles, for kitchens, halls and the like, which have to put up with spillages and muddy feet. Wood floors are the latest competitor to fitted carpets, not only for their looks and practicality, but also because they don't harbour dust and irritating mites as carpet does.

WALL-TO-WALL LUXURY

Carpet is still the biggest-selling floor covering around. Most people start by looking for a colour or pattern they like, but what matters more is how well the carpet will wear. This depends on how the carpet was made, and on what type of fibres it contains.

Woven carpets are made by the Axminster or Wilton methods, and have fibre tufts stitched into a coarse fabric backing. Tufted carpets, which are usually cheaper than woven ones, have the tufts stuck to the backing. Both are laid over a foam underlay to make them softer under foot (and to make them wear longer, so don't think you'll save money by skipping the underlay). You can get cheap carpets with a foam backing stuck to them, but they're worth considering only for rooms you don't use much, such as a spare bedroom. The best fibre mix for most rooms is 80 per cent wool and 20 per cent synthetic fibre, usually nylon. Go for all-synthetic fibres in 'wet' areas such as bathrooms, halls and kitchens.

Above all, check the carpet's wear rating. You need a light domestic grade for bedrooms, medium domestic for areas of average wear, such as dining rooms, general domestic for living rooms, and heavy domestic for halls, stairs and landings.

Most carpet is still made in imperial 9 ft (2.75 m) and 12 ft (3.65 m) widths, but the metric 4 m (13 ft) width is now becoming more common. You buy carpet by the linear yard or metre. Always take room measurements (and ideally a floor plan) with you when you go shopping as mistakes can be very expensive.

STILL ON THE ROLL

The other big seller in sheet floor coverings is sheet vinyl. This is made by printing the design on a layer of plastic and covering it with a clear wear layer. On the more expensive types, a cushioned backing layer is added to make the floor feel warmer and softer under foot.

A huge choice of patterns and designs is available,

carpet

vinyl tiles

cork tiles

sheet vinyl flooring

wood flooring

ranging from imitations of floor tiles and woodstrip effects to striking modern patterns. Sheet vinyl is sold by the metre from rolls in widths of 2 m (6 ft 6 in), 3 m (10 ft) and 4 m (13 ft).

Lino, short for linoleum, is making a big comeback after going out of fashion when sheet vinyl came along in the 1960s. It's no longer the boring, traditional product of old. New designs and colourways, plus the fact that you can cut and fit different colours together to create your own unique floor covering, make it the hard flooring with a difference.

THE PICK OF THE TILES

If you prefer tiles on your floors, you have a choice of four main types. Ceramic floor tiles come in nearly as many colours and designs as their wall tile relatives, and in some very interesting shapes alongside the usual squares and rectangles. They're thicker than wall tiles, and usually have a softer surface glaze so that they're not dangerously slippery underfoot.

Quarry tiles are unglazed ceramic tiles, made in a range of attractive red, brown and buff shades. They can be laid with standard tile adhesive – much less messy than the traditional cement mortar – but need sealing once down if they're not to become stained in use. Most quarry tiles are made in 100 mm (4 in) or 150 mm (6 in) squares.

Vinyl tiles are basically squares or rectangles of sheet vinyl which you stick to the floor. Most are self-adhesive. They're relatively inexpensive, easier to handle than sheet vinyl in rooms that have lots of obstructions, such as bathrooms and WCs, and are just as waterproof and hard-wearing. Most vinyl tiles measure 300 mm (12 in) square and are sold in packs of six or nine tiles, but

other sizes are available in the more expensive ranges.

Cork tiles are squares or rectangles of compressed cork bark, also intended to be stuck to the floor and usually self-adhesive. Cheaper tiles are unsealed, and need two or three coats of varnish once they've been laid. More expensive ones come ready-sealed and can be walked on as soon as you've laid them. They're usually 300 mm (12 in) square, about 6 mm (¼ in) thick and much denser than cork wall tiles, so don't buy the wrong type.

WOOD FLOORS

Decorative wood floors have been popular for centuries, and sanded-and-sealed floorboards have always been fashionable. But laying a decorative planked floor over existing floors creates a perfectly smooth surface that's both stunning to look at and very comfortable under foot. The planks are tongued and grooved, and are stuck together as they're laid to make a complete 'floating' floor. Cheaper floors are laminated, while more expensive types are solid wood. A range of woods is available, from beech and light oak to dark mahogany. Plank and pack sizes vary from brand to brand, so check before you buy to estimate how much you need.

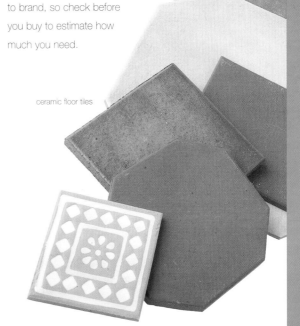

ceramic floor tiles

decorating tools

It's surprising how many bits of equipment you need to do decorating properly. Some are inexpensive and their quality doesn't matter much, but there are two things on which it pays to spend money: good paintbrushes and a professional-quality tile-cutting jig. As for the rest of your decorating equipment, simply buy the best you can afford. Here's what you'll need.

PAINTING TOOLS

You can put paint on with a brush, a roller or a pad. Brushes are best for woodwork (a roller is only useful on a flush door and shelving anyway), but the choice is yours for walls and ceilings. Brushing can be tiring work, because you need a wide brush to get along quickly, and the wider the brush, the more it drags. Rollers are speedy, but cleaning the sleeves afterwards can be time-consuming. Pads are good because they apply paint quickly and evenly, they don't waste as much paint as a roller does, and they're much easier to clean.

You need brushes in several sizes. Start with a 100 mm (4 in) brush for walls and ceilings, a 50 mm (2 in) brush for general woodwork and a 25 mm (1 in) brush for the fiddly bits. It's also worth buying a 12 mm (½ in) cutting-in brush, which has its bristles cut at an angle. This is better than a straight-cut brush for painting round glass and getting into other awkward angles. Buy a plastic paint kettle, too, so you don't contaminate the paint in the original can as you work.

Rollers come in two standard widths – 180 mm (7 in) and 230 mm (9 in). Buy a roller with a wire cage to take the sleeve, and pick a short-pile sleeve for smooth

paintbrush

roller tray

paint roller

paint kettle

paint roller

mini-roller

paint pad

surfaces and a long-pile sleeve for textured ones. You'll
also need a plastic roller tray to hold the paint and let you
load the sleeve. Add a slimline radiator roller if you want to
paint behind your central heating fittings.

Pads are best bought in a kit. You usually get a large
wall pad, a smaller woodwork pad and a slim wad for
small areas, plus a plastic tray to hold the paint and let
you load the pads.

PAPER-HANGING TOOLS

Hanging wallpaper needs a lot of tools. Let's run
through the operations step by step so you can make
up a shopping list. First, you have to mix up the paste,
so you'll need a clean bucket, a measuring jug and a
stirrer (a wooden kitchen spoon is ideal). Next, you
have to measure and cut the paper, so you need a
tape measure, pencil, straightedge and either scissors
or a sharp trimming knife. You'll need scissors anyway
to trim the paper to length when you've hung it, so buy
a pair of proper long-bladed paper-hanging shears.
Don't use household scissors. Then you have to apply
the paste, so you'll need a fold-away pasting table and
a paste brush, although a clean 100 mm (4 in)
paintbrush will do at a pinch. If hanging a ready-pasted
paper, scrap the tools for mixing and applying the
paste, and buy a plastic soaking trough instead.

Now it's paper-hanging time. For a start, you need a
plumb bob and line to mark a vertical guideline on the
wall – essential to keep everything straight and true.
Get a chalk line, too, if you plan to paper any ceilings,
so you can also mark a guideline there. You need a
proper paper-hanging brush to smooth the paper into
place as you work. You can get away with using a
sponge instead if you're hanging washables, vinyls or
ready-pasted wallpaper, but a brush is the better all-
round tool for perfect results. Last but not least, it's
well worth having a seam roller, which you run along
adjoining lengths of paper to make sure they stick
down well.

paste bucket
paste brush
paper hanging brush
sponge
seam roller
chalk line
pasting trough
trimming guide
plumb bob and line
wallpaper
trimmers
tape measure

TILING TOOLS

You don't need nearly so many tools to do ceramic tiling.
Start with a good-quality tile-cutting jig, which will earn
its cost by not wasting any tiles through the inaccurate
cutting or unexpected breakages that a pencil tile cutter
always seems to cause. The jig will also cut floor tiles,
which a pencil cutter won't. The only time it's worth
having a pencil tile-cutter is if you're tackling just one
small-scale job – a basin splash-back, say – and you
can't justify the cost of buying the jig.

You'll need a toothed plastic adhesive spreader to apply
the tile adhesive on. A small one is usually supplied with
every tub of adhesive, but a wider one will speed up the job.
Add a proper, rubber-edged grout squeegee for grouting the
gaps between the tiles. Lastly, for those awkward cuts
around pipes, switches and socket outlets, nothing beats a
tile saw. Forget about nibbling away the waste with pincers
or pliers: it doesn't work nearly as well as a saw.

If you're laying vinyl or cork tiles, all you'll need is a
tape measure, a sharp trimming knife, a felt-tip pen and
a 610 mm (2 ft) steel ruler. A chalk line is useful for
setting out the tiles, but it isn't essential. Use some
scrap board as a cutting mat. Vinyl and cork tiles also
require an adhesive spreader, unless you're laying the
self-adhesive variety.

decorating sundries

Once the painting, paper-hanging and tiling tools have been sorted out, you need to think about the problem of reaching what you're decorating – and that doesn't mean perching precariously on a dining chair. You need some proper access equipment. You'll also need tools and equipment for preparation, too, and the stuff you always seem to run out of when the shops are closed – fillers, sandpaper, adhesives and so on.

REACHING THE HEIGHTS

One thing you can't do without is a lightweight, folding aluminium stepladder. Get one with seven treads, a top handrail and a flat-top platform that's wide enough to take a paint roller tray or your power drill. An alternative that's worth considering if you have to decorate the stairwell is a folding multi-purpose ladder. You can set this up in various ways so that it can stand on the floor, rest on the stair-treads or act as a low-level platform with a plank laid on top of it for painting ceilings.

If you're papering ceilings, you really need a work platform that can span the room so you can walk the length of each strip of paper without hopping dangerously from chair to chair. Head for your local hire shop and pick up some decorator's trestles and lightweight staging.

hot air gun

orbital sander

TACKLING THE PREPARATION

Whether you're planning to redecorate walls, ceilings or woodwork, you won't get decent results unless you spend some time on the preparation. Any surface will benefit from a wash down with sugar soap (an abrasive detergent that leaves a rough surface to grip the paint) or household detergent. Gloss paint needs sanding lightly to key the surface for the new paint and to remove any bits left on the surface from the last time you painted, so you need abrasive paper or an all-in-one sanding block. Dents and cracks need filling, so you'll need wood and plaster fillers, plus some decorator's mastic and a cartridge gun for tackling those cracks that keep reopening along skirting boards and where walls meet ceilings.

The tools you'll need include filling knives (which have flexible blades), a paint scraper and a wallpaper scraper (which have rigid blades), and a cunning tool called a combination shavehook for stripping paint from mouldings. You can strip paint with chemical paint stripper or an electric hot-air gun, while a hired steam stripper will make light work of removing painted or washable wallpaper. A power sander will quickly smooth both wood and plaster surfaces after you've done any

necessary filling. Lastly, a brick bolster and a club
hammer are the ideal tools for knocking off old
ceramic tiles.

STICKING THINGS

The final basketful of stuff you'll need to buy includes
some adhesives to stick whatever you're using to
whatever you're decorating. For paper-hanging, you
need wallpaper paste – either in powder form for you to
mix up, or ready-mixed in a tub. Ready-mixed is
expensive, but is recommended for certain heavyweight
papers and for wall fabrics. Make sure you buy paste
containing a fungicide if you're hanging washable or vinyl
paper, since the paste dries slowly under their plastic
surfaces and black mould can grow in it, spoiling your
new decorations. Pick a pack that will make enough
paste for the number of rolls you're hanging, plus a
bit over.

You need special border adhesive (also in a tub) to
stick borders and friezes to washable and vinyl paper;

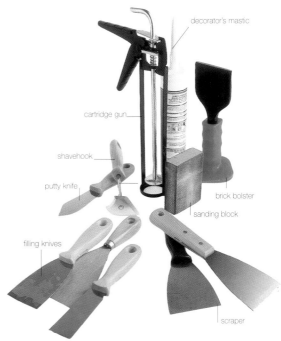

decorator's mastic

cartridge gun

shavehook

putty knife

brick bolster

sanding block

filling knives

scraper

adhesive

wire wool

masking tape

sponge

LAMINATED FL

UniBond
ALL PURPOSE
WATERPROOF
WALL TILE ADHESIVE & GROUT

EVO-STIK
Wood Adhesive
Extra Fast

RAWLPLUG
PLASTIC WOOD

abrasives

tile spacers

ordinary wallpaper paste simply won't stick to their
waterproof surfaces. For the same reason, with these two
paper types you'll also have to use overlap adhesive to
stick down the inevitable overlaps at room corners.

On to tiling. Here you'll need ceramic wall tile
adhesive and grout, which comes in a tub and does
both the sticking and the grouting. Pick a waterproof
type for use in bathrooms. Get a pack of tile spacers
too – small plastic crosses that fit at each tile corner as
you work and keep your tiling gaps uniform. If tiling a
floor, you need ceramic floor tile adhesive and a
separate pack of grout – again, use the waterproof
variety for bathrooms. For sheet vinyl and on adhesive
floor tiles, there's special flooring adhesive, and for
laying wood floors you'll need ordinary PVA wood
adhesive. Buy all these products as and when you
need them, and buy no more than necessary for the
job. They don't keep well, and nothing is more
annoying than finding a tub or tube that's set hard
when you try to use it again in the future.

wood and man-made boards

Wood in one form or another is the basic raw material for all sorts of DIY projects. You're likely to use both natural timber and one or more of the various man-made boards. MDF (medium-density fibreboard) is the new DIY woodworker's favourite, knocking chipboard off the No. 1 spot for making things such as shelving and simple furniture, while ordinary softwood does just about anything you want it to.

THE NATURAL STUFF

Wood comes in two main types. There's softwood, which comes from evergreen trees (conifers) such as pine and larch, and there's hardwood, which comes from just about everything else and includes oak, beech, teak and mahogany. Softwoods aren't all soft and hardwoods aren't all hard – the balsa tree, for example, is a hardwood. The two categories are simply a botanist's way of classifying trees. You'll be using softwood most of the time; unless you're a budding cabinet-maker, the only hardwoods you'll come across are used for making decorative timber mouldings.

Softwood is very pale in colour, with slightly darker stripes, which are the tree's annual growth rings. Look at the end of a length of wood, and you can see these quite clearly. If the grain lines are straight and parallel to the face or edge of the wood, it will be quite stable and won't warp in use, but if they're steeply curved, the wood might curl up (called 'cupping' in the trade) and twist along its length. When you buy any softwood, always inspect each length to check that it is straight and true. Reject any that are curved or twisted. Look out for dead knots too – they mark where branches were and can shrink and fall out.

UNDERSTANDING WOOD SIZES

Wood is first sawn to a range of standard metric sizes, then planed smooth. You're unlikely to need any sawn wood; it's used mainly for things such as floor joists and the framework inside timber partition walls. Planed wood is what you'll be using for your DIY projects.

Now here comes the confusing bit. Wood is labelled by its sawn size – 50 x 25 mm (2 x 1 in), for example – but the planing process removes 2–3 mm (up to ⅛ in) of wood from each face of the length. So your piece of two by one – as everyone still calls it – might end up measuring only 44 x 21 mm (1¾ x ⅞ in). This is its actual size; the 50 x 25 mm measurement is its nominal size.

This matters a lot when you're making something such as a square frame in 50 x 25 mm wood with simple butt corner joints (see pages 100–103). If the frame sides are each 610 mm (2 ft) long, you might expect to cut two

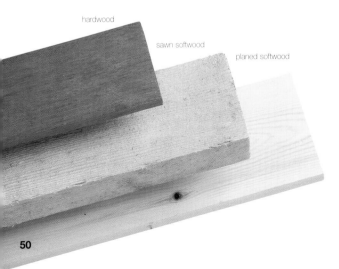

hardwood

sawn softwood

planed softwood

pieces to that length, and the other two to 510 – 610 mm, less twice the width of the wood, which you thought was 50 mm (2 in). Wrong! The two shorter sides would have to measure 522 mm – 610 mm less 2 x 44 mm – to give you a frame 610 mm square. The golden rule in a situation like this is always to measure the actual size of the wood, not to go by its nominal size.

Softwood comes in standard lengths – usually 1.8 or 2.4 m (just under 6 ft and 8 ft respectively) – in the DIY sheds. Many of them have the annoying habit of selling all but the largest wood sizes in packs containing several lengths, which might be far more than you need. Their prices are also on the high side. You can buy wood in lengths that are any multiple of 300 mm (just under 12 in) from timber merchants; you won't have to buy a pack of several lengths if you don't need that much wood, and the price per length will be quite a bit less than in the sheds. So it'll pay to get to know your local merchant if you use wood regularly.

FOUR BOARDS

There are four main types of man-made board – plywood, chipboard, hardboard and MDF. Each has different pros and cons.

Plywood is made by sticking thin layers (veneers) of wood together, with the grain in each layer running at right angles to the grain in its neighbours. It comes in sheets ranging from 3 mm (⅛ in) up to 18 mm (¾ in) thick. It's strong, but the edges splinter as you cut it and they need careful finishing. You're most likely to use it for jobs such as covering the sides of built-in cupboards with a timber framework. It also makes an excellent base for ceramic floor tiles.

Chipboard is made by bonding small chips of wood together with a mixture of wood dust and adhesive. This is done under pressure to create a sheet that's stable, but heavy and not very strong – chipboard shelves are notorious for bowing when loaded – and the edges are also difficult to finish neatly. Worse still, the resin in

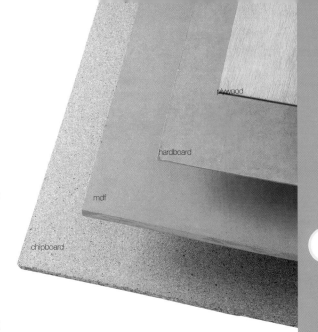

chipboard blunts cutting tools very quickly. The commonest thicknesses are 12 and 18 mm (½ and ¾ in). Chipboard is used less often now that MDF has come along.

Hardboard is thin and relatively weak board made by pressing wood fibres and resins together. The commonest thickness is 3 mm (⅛ in), and it's used mainly for jobs such as boxing in pipes, forming the back panels of cupboards and covering bumpy floorboards when you're laying smooth floor coverings.

MDF is the ideal sheet material for most DIY jobs, from shelving and making cupboards to panelling around the bath. It's a thicker, stronger sort of hardboard, with a smooth surface that's excellent for painting but very thirsty: use a layer of primer to seal the surface first. Inside it has a uniform texture that cuts and drills easily to leave clean, smooth edges needing very little finishing. It comes in 6 mm, 12 mm and 18 mm (¼, ½ and ¾ in) thicknesses. Its only drawback? It's about twice the price of chipboard. But it's at least twice as nice to use.

BOARD SIZES

All these boards come in standard sheets measuring 2440 x 1220 mm (8 x 4 ft) – far too big to carry home easily, but the most economical size to buy. Most timber stockists also sell smaller panels. The commonest are 1827 x 607 mm (6 x 2 ft) and 1220 x 607 mm (4 x 2 ft) – both small enough to tuck under your arm.

the essential toolkit

If your DIY ambitions extend beyond the occasional bit of painting and decorating, you're going to need some more tools. In fact, you'll have bought and used some of them already, such as a steel tape measure and a trimming knife – one to measure wallpaper and the other to cut it. This following assortment of extras will enable you to tackle quite a few more simple DIY jobs.

DRILLING THINGS

Lots of jobs involve making holes for fixings of one sort or another. The best tool to buy for this is a power drill. Make sure it has variable speed and optional hammer action so that you can drill holes in solid walls and floors as well as in wood and metal. The power of drills is measured by the motor wattage; a drill rated at 500W will cope with just about anything you ask of it. If possible, choose a model that comes with a case so that you can store the drill away neatly when not being used.

You'll also need two sorts of drill bits – one lot for wood and the other for masonry. The twist drill bits for wood look dark grey and dull and the masonry drill bits look silvery and have a cutting tip that is brazed. Buy a set of steel twist drill bits in a plastic (or better still, metal) storage case so that they don't rattle around loose in your tool box. Buy just one size of masonry drill bit, to match whatever wallplugs you normally use – probably the 6 mm or 6.5 mm (¼ in) size – and replace it when it gets blunt. Don't waste your money on a set containing sizes you'll never use.

FIXING THINGS

You must have a hammer, and to start with the most useful will be a small pin hammer. This will bang in panel pins and small nails to hold joints together, and will also do other odd jobs, such as tapping wallplugs into drilled holes in walls.

You can never have too many screwdrivers, but three will get you started. The first should be a screwdriver for screws with slotted heads. Pick one with a comfortable, soft-grip handle, and a blade about 125 mm (5 in) long and 5mm (just under ¼ in) wide. The second is for cross-head (Pozidriv) screws; ask for a No. 2 Pozidriver, which will cope with most common screw sizes of this type. Don't forget to buy a bradawl, which is used for making the pilot hole in wood before you start driving a screw in. Its slim screwdriver-like tip can also be used at a pinch for driving or undoing the smallest screws.

CUTTING THINGS

You already have a trimming knife. If it's the type that takes double-ended blades, you can buy a small saw blade for it and fit that instead. This will cut wood up to about 50 x 25 mm (2 x 1 in) in cross-section. If you want to cut thicker stuff, get a tenon saw. This has a blade about 250 mm (10 in) long, and has a strip of metal running along the top edge of the blade to keep it rigid.

To help you mark and cut wood square with your saw, you need a tool called a try square. It has a flat steel blade fixed at exactly 90 degrees to its handle. You hold the handle against the edge of the wood, and mark the cutting line on it by running your pencil along one edge of the blade.

MAKING JOINTS

If you're planning to make anything in wood, you'll have to cut some simple joints, and for these you'll need two or three different-sized wood chisels. Buy ones with bevelled (sloping) edges to the blades. They cut into corners more easily than blades with square edges. You'll also need an oilstone and a small can of household oil so that you can re-sharpen the blade when it gets blunt.

Make sure you have a good supply of sandpaper for smoothing wood once you've finished sawing and chiselling it. You can buy packs containing fine, medium and coarse grades.

STAYING ON THE LEVEL

There's one little tool that's essential for any job that involves getting things truly horizontal (such as a shelf) or vertical (such as a length of wallpaper). It's a spirit level, and a short one with two bubbles will do the job perfectly. You can team it up with a straight length of wood to draw long lines on walls.

KEEPING THINGS TIDY

Buy yourself a plastic or metal tool box to keep all your kit in so that you can find your tools when you need them. Most boxes have small internal compartments that are ideal for storing nails, screws, wallplugs and other bits and pieces. Keep the box indoors if you can so that steel tools don't rust in the damp air of your shed or garage.

try square
trimming knife
tape measure
drill
spirit level
screwdriver
tenon saw
wood chisels
Pozidriver
abrasives
pin hammer
bradawl

fixings and hardware

You'll need fixings – nails and screws – to hold things together and to attach them to various surfaces around your house. Screws need something for their threads to grip when used to fix things to walls and ceilings. Plastic wallplugs are best suited to solid walls, while cavity fixings of one sort or another are needed for plasterboard partition walls and for ceilings. Let's do nails first.

panel pins

lost head nails

round wire nails

masonry nails

SMALL NAILS, BIG NAILS

The nail you'll find most useful isn't called a nail at all: it's the panel pin, and as its name implies, it pins panels to their supporting framework. It can also fix slim mouldings to furniture, hold small joints together and attach timber cladding to its wooden support battens. Panel pins come in various sizes, from 15 mm (⅝ in) upwards. The 25 mm (1 in) size will do for most jobs. You need something a bit bigger for fixing things such as architraves around door frames, and for securing joints in wood too thick for panel pins. Go for some lost-head nails, which have a cone-shaped head you can punch into the wood surface with a pin punch, then hide with wood filler. Again, a range of sizes is available, but the 50 mm (2 in) one will be the most useful all-rounder to buy.

The third type of nail required is suitable for nailing up frameworks that will be hidden by cladding or panelling. It's the round wire nail, which has a round, flat head that remains visible on the wood surface, making a pretty secure fixing as nails go. Sizes range from 25 mm (1 in) up to 150 mm (6 in) in length; buy whichever size you need for the job you're tackling.

If you want to fix wood to solid masonry, the quickest way of doing so is to use masonry nails. These specially hardened nails penetrate bricks and blocks, and even concrete, so long as you don't hit a hidden stone inside. You need a claw hammer to drive them in. Sizes range from 25 mm upwards; buy them long enough to pass through whatever you're fixing and then to penetrate the wall to a depth of at least 40 mm (1½ in).

SCREWS FOR EXTRA GRIP

Nails can pull out under loads unless the joint they're securing is glued as well. Screws can't pull out because their spiral threads grip fast in the wood. The other advantage they have over nails is that they can be undone just as easily as they were screwed in in the first place. Most are plain steel, but you can also get them with bright plated or black finishes and in decorative brass.

There are two main types of screws, which are distinguished by the way their heads are shaped. Slot-head screws have a straight groove running right across the head, and are driven in with a flat-bladed screwdriver. Cross-head screws have a cross-shaped recess in the head, and are driven with a special cross-point screwdriver. Most woodscrews have a Pozidriv recess, and are driven with a Pozidriv screwdriver. Many screws on appliances have a Phillips recess, which differs slightly from a Pozidriv one. A Phillips screwdriver will drive both types, but a Pozidriver won't fit into a Phillips recess.

For fixing wood, it's normal to use countersunk screws. They have a cone-shaped underside to the head, designed to sit in a matching countersunk hole drilled in the wood so that the screw head finishes up lying flush with the wood surface.

Screws come in lots of different lengths and diameters. The diameter is called the screw gauge, and is a simple number. For most DIY jobs you'll need screws in gauge numbers 6, 8 and 10. The most useful sizes to buy are 25, 38 and 50 mm (1, 1½ and 2 in).

MAKING WALL FIXINGS

Screws won't hold in solid masonry, even if you drill them a hole. You have to line the hole with something that will grip the screw threads and the sides of the hole. It's called a wallplug. To use one, check on the plug's packaging to see what size masonry drill bit you need to use. Drill the appropriate sized hole, then tap in the plug and drive the screw into it: again, the packaging will tell you what screw gauge you should use.

When it comes to making fixings into plasterboard walls and ceilings, you have a different problem. Once the screw's gone through the thin plasterboard, it's in thin air, so you have to provide some sort of anchor that will hold the screw and also grip the plasterboard. For lightweight fixings, such as a soap dish, use a self-drill fixing, which you simply screw into a pilot hole in the board, then drive in the fixing screw.

For medium loads, use plastic cavity wall fixings instead. You push the closed-up fixing through a hole in the plasterboard, then drive in the screw. As the screw passes through of the fixing, the tip of the plastic is pulled towards the surface and forms two projecting wings that grip the inner face of the board. A heavier-duty metal type with four wings and its own special screw will support quite heavy loads, such as bookshelves, especially when several are needed to support it.

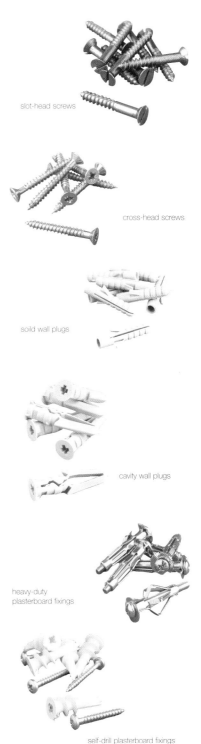

slot-head screws

cross-head screws

soild wall plugs

cavity wall plugs

heavy-duty
plasterboard fixings

self-drill plasterboard fixings

more tools for your tool box

As you get better at DIY, you'll find you need more tools. You'll get the most help from adding some extra power tools to your armoury, because they do everything hand tools do but twice as well and three times as quickly. However, there are also some hand tools and bits of equipment you might want to get hold of too.

power tool safety

- When using a power tool, avoid wearing loose-fitting clothing, a tie or a necklace as they could all get caught in the moving parts of the tool. Tie long hair back or gather it up under a cap.
- Always switch off and unplug the tool before fitting any attachments, or adjusting the tool settings.
- Double-check that drill bits, saw blades and the like are securely fitted before turning the tool on.
- Use attachments and accessories designed especially for your power tool.
- Never bypass the use of any safety guards; they're designed to protect you from injury.
- Use a suitable extension lead if you need to work away from a power source. Uncoil it fully to prevent the flex overheating on the reel. Never pick a power tool up by its flex.

MORE POWER TO YOUR ELBOW

The first thing to add to your tool kit is a jigsaw. This takes the hard work out of sawing both wood and man-made boards, and will cope with all but the most delicate cuts (it's back to the tenon saw for those). With its tilting soleplate, it will also make cuts at angles other than 90 degrees – handy for cutting neat 45-degree mitres on the ends of skirting boards, for example. The most versatile of all jigsaws is called a scrolling saw. This has a knob on the top of the saw body, which you use to control the blade direction as you work. There are different blades for cutting wood, man-made boards, plastic and metal, so buy a selection and you'll be ready for anything.

If you think sawing is hard work, you've never done sanding – at least, not on large areas. A power sander will change all that. Go for an orbital sander with a rectangular baseplate if most of your sanding work involves finishing planed wood or smooth boards. One that can be connected via a hose and adaptor to a cylinder vacuum cleaner will help keep the dust down. You can also get smaller sanders with triangular-shaped sanding plates, which are great for sanding right into awkward corners.

Sometimes you need wood that isn't close to the standard sizes in the shops, or you have to tackle a job such as shortening a door slightly so that it will clear your new floor covering. A power planer is the answer. It will effortlessly remove as much wood as you want. When the blade gets blunt, you simply fit a replacement and carry on planing.

A power router is the tool that will give you the most fun. You drive it along edges and across the surface of wood or boards, creating grooves and ornate edges that give your work a seriously professional look. The drive shaft can be fitted with a huge range of differently shaped cutters, and you can get all sorts

cordless drill

sliding bevel

router

power planer

gripping pliers

scrolling jigsaw

G–cramps

mitre block

orbital sander

of accessories such as guide fences (for making long, straight cuts) and trammel bars (for working in circles) to make your router even more versatile.

The last power tool that's worth its weight in gold is a cordless drill. This lets you drill holes and drive screws when you're nowhere near a power point, and models with hammer action will make holes in walls as well as woodwork. Go for one with a battery rating of 9.6 volts so that you get plenty of power, and invest in a spare battery.

BITS AND PIECES

Working safely with tools – especially power tools – means securing whatever you're working on to your workbench. What you need are some cramps (also known as clamps). You can buy the traditional G-cramps illustrated here, or fast-action types that you can set and release in a second with one hand. If you want to clamp up furniture, or stick planks together edge to edge, head for your local hire shop and ask for some sash cramps. They're too expensive to buy for that one-off job.

Not all the cuts you want to make will be right-angled ones. For example, 45-degree mitre cuts are needed to form neat corners on picture frames or the architrave

mouldings that go around door openings. A simple device called a mitre block will guide your tenon saw accurately. And if you need to match an unusual angle, a tool called a sliding bevel will do the trick. You set its blade at the angle you want to copy, then place its handle against the wood you're working on and mark the angle on to it. It works a bit like a try square, but can cope with any angle you want.

Lastly, there's a tool that's so useful you'll wonder how you ever managed without it. It's a pair of gripping pliers, and is a cross between ordinary pliers and a small cramp. You can set the jaws to a range of different widths, then lock them into place to hold things together and give you a third hand while you work. Brilliant!

TEN TOOLS TO THINK ABOUT

Here's a quick checklist of some other tools you might find worth adding to your tool box.

1 A claw hammer   **6** A staple gun

2 A pin punch   **7** A cartridge gun

3 More screwdrivers   **8** A hole saw

4 A pair of pliers   **9** A dowelling device

5 An adjustable spanner   **10** A portable workbench

decorating and diy

By the time you reach this part of the book, I hope you'll have had a good look round your home and worked out what you want to do with it. You'll also know a fair bit by now about the various decorating and DIY tools and materials you'll be using.

Now it's time to get cracking with some real DIY jobs, and I'll begin with the decorating because that's what most home-owners are prepared to tackle themselves, even if they choose to leave other jobs to the professionals.

Everyone can use a paintbrush, can't they? And hanging wallpaper is a doddle, isn't it? Well, you can actually get yourself into a fair old mess with most DIY jobs if you don't know what you're doing. So all the way through this chapter you'll find clear, step-by-step instructions that take you through the job from start to finish, quick-reference checklists to help you get together everything needed for the job, and tips that really work to help you save time and effort and get top-quality results. If, despite all that, it still goes pear-shaped, look out for my Lifesaver boxes. They'll get you back on the straight and narrow in next to no time.

planning your decorating

Planning sounds boring but, believe me, it saves time in the long run. It helps you think the job through, make all those difficult decisions about colour-scheming, and get together everything you need before you start work.

THINK BUDGET

If you're going to redecorate a room, begin by deciding how far you're going to go. Will you just repaint the walls, ceiling and woodwork? Will you be papering the walls for the first time, or do you want to replace the paper you already have? And how about changing the carpet and curtains, even the upholstery and the lighting? These decisions will often depend on the size of your budget. You can probably do a quick room repaint for £50, but add some new wallpaper and you'll at least double the spend. More extensive changes than this will definitely have you dipping deep into your savings. The choice is yours, of course, but be sure you know what you're in for before you start.

START A FILE

Unless you like white rooms, you'll need paint colour charts, wallpaper and even fabric samples to help you decide which products to use. You can pick up free colour charts from the DIY sheds, and most of them have unwrapped rolls of wallpaper and borders on display, so you can tear off samples. You might need to go further afield for fabric samples: try the curtain shops and department stores in your local high street. Don't forget local markets, which can be an excellent source of cheap fabrics. Then buy a cardboard pocket file from a stationer's to keep everything in.

One of the best ways of getting colour-scheming ideas is from the many monthly home magazines now available. Whenever you see something you like – a whole room makeover, or just a handful of interesting details – tear the page out and put it in your file. When you do this, check to see whether all the relevant product details are on that page or elsewhere in the magazine; many print separate lists of stockists at the back, so it's useful to tear those out and clip the pages together as well. There's nothing more annoying than knowing what you want but not where to get it!

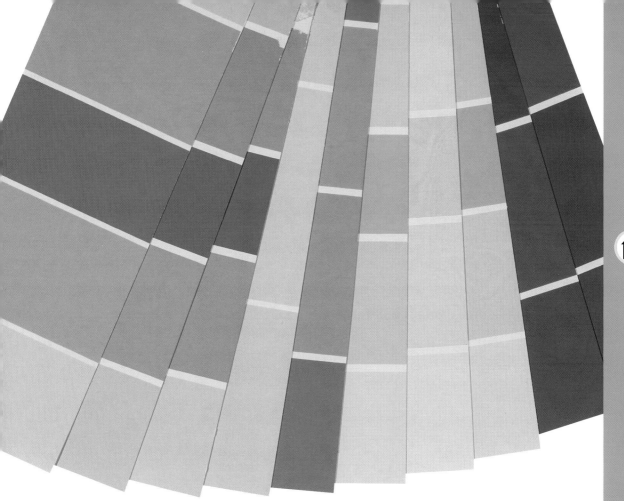

PLAN YOUR TIME

Your time is the free ingredient of any project, but you still have to work out how much of it is needed for the job. Don't underestimate how long things can take. Just preparing a room for redecorating – clearing the furniture, taking everything off the walls, washing down surfaces, patching up any damage, covering up the carpet or stripping it and so on – could take a day at least. Allow a whole weekend for a simple repaint, and two if you're paper-hanging, tiling or laying new flooring as well. This might sound a lot, but you'll feel much better if you set yourself a realistic timetable and are able to keep to it as you go along. Everyone hates a job that drifts on and on when you thought you could be done in a day.

READ THROUGH THE JOB

Last but not least, make sure you know exactly what you're up against by reading through whichever bits of this chapter apply to the job you're tackling. For example, a bathroom make-over could involve replacing all the old wall tiles (or tiling over them, see page 90), painting the ceiling and the woodwork (see pages 74–9) and putting down some new cork tiles (see page 94). You could even fix that annoying dripping tap (see page 158) while you're at it.

By doing this now, you'll be able to work out what order to do things in and then organize your shopping and work time accordingly. For this particular job, you should do tiling (the messiest bit) first, then painting and finally flooring. But before you can begin work, you have to estimate how much of everything you need…

estimating materials

Decorating materials are not cheap. Accurate estimating is all about having enough stuff to finish the job, with perhaps 5 per cent extra as a margin for error. You can keep any leftovers in case you have to touch up or replace bits that get marked or damaged in the future.

PAINT ESTIMATES

Here's a guide to how far you can expect different paints to go. But remember that coverage depends on two things – how thickly you slap it on, and how porous the surface is. As a general rule, two thin coats give better coverage than a single thick one, and you won't get so many messy drips and runs either. And if you're painting bare plaster or plasterboard, which really soak paint up, expect to use half as much paint again as you would on a surface that's been painted before. Finally, always check the coverage on the tin you're buying in case it differs from the figures below and, if it does, use those figures in your sums.

Liquid gloss	16 sq m (170 sq ft) per litre
Non-drip gloss	13 sq m (140 sq ft) per litre
Eggshell	12 sq m (130 sq ft) per litre
Matt emulsion	15 sq m (160 sq ft) per litre
Silk emulsion	14 sq m (150 sq ft) per litre
Non-drip emulsion	12 sq m (130 sq ft) per litre
Primer/undercoat	11 sq m (120 sq ft) per litre
Varnish	15 sq m (160 sq ft) per litre

top tip

When buying wall paper, always check that all the rolls have the same batch number printed on the label. This eliminates the risk of any slight colour variations between rolls. It's well worth buying an extra roll as insurance against making a mistake with the estimating, since the batch you buy from may have been exhausted if you have to go back later for another roll. You can always return it for a refund if you find you don't need it.

WALLPAPER ESTIMATES

Measure your floor-to-ceiling height, and check that you will be able to get four lengths out of each standard 10.05 m (33 ft) roll of paper. A large pattern repeat or a ceiling over 2.4 m (8 ft) high can mean getting only three lengths per roll. Then measure the perimeter of the room, ignoring door and window openings, unless they amount to more than about 10 per cent of the total perimeter.

A standard roll of wallpaper is 520 mm (20½ in) wide, so if you double the room's perimeter measurement (taken in metres), that will tell you how many lengths of wallpaper the room will need. Divide that by 4 (or 3 in high-ceilinged rooms) to work out how many rolls will be required.

Wall height (in metres)	Measurement around room (in metres)											
	9	10	11	12	13	14	15	16	17	18	19	20
2 to 2.2	4	4	5	5	5	6	6	6	6	7	7	8
2.2 to 2.4	4	4	5	5	6	6	6	7	7	8	8	9
2.4 to 2.6	4	5	5	6	6	7	7	8	8	9	9	10
2.6 to 2.8	5	5	6	6	7	7	8	8	9	9	10	11
2.8 to 3	5	5	6	7	7	8	8	9	9	10	11	12

Use the table above as a rough guide to the number of rolls you will need, assuming that you can get four lengths of wallpaper out of each roll.

For ceilings, measure the length of one strip and count how many strips will be needed. Calculate how many strips you can cut from each 10.05 m (33 ft) roll, then work out how many rolls you will need from that.

Depending on the room dimensions, you may find it less wasteful to hang short lengths across the room, rather than long lengths down it. Check the lengths-per-roll arithmetic to see which is the better option.

TILE ESTIMATES

Most packs of wall and floor tiles tell you how many square metres they'll cover, so it's easy to work out how many you need. But if they don't, make a note of the tile size you've chosen and how many you get in a pack. Then count up how many will fill a row across the area you're tiling, and how many rows you'll need. Multiply the two figures together to get the total number of tiles you'll need, then work out how many packs that represents. It's as simple as that.

SHEET FLOORING ESTIMATES

Unless you're simply buying an offcut of carpet, vinyl or whatever to put in the downstairs loo, it's always best to leave the estimating of sheet flooring to your supplier, because mistakes can be expensive and then they won't be your fault! Measure up the room concerned, then draw a sketch plan that shows features such as alcoves, bay windows and so on. Hand that to the salesman and let him work out how much you need.

using access equipment

You will need proper access equipment to reach ceilings and the tops of walls comfortably and safely when you're decorating or repairing them. Don't improvise by balancing on chairs or standing on boxes. Fall off, and you'll have paint everywhere, and possibly a serious injury into the bargain.

STEPS

A decent stepladder is a must. Pick a lightweight aluminium type with five treads, a flat top platform for putting tools on (*not* for standing on) and a top handrail. Make sure its locks are engaged when it's open. Buy two identical stepladders plus a 2.4 m (8 ft) scaffold board (or hire the board from a local hire shop) and you can set up a platform that's ideal for painting walls or ceilings.

When using steps, set them up so that they stand square and level. If you have to stretch sideways from them, keep your hips within the sides of the steps and keep both feet on the treads all the time. Don't lean out sideways too far, or you could topple over. And take care when you step off that you don't trip over power-tool flexes or put your foot in the paste bucket. We've all done it...

LADDERS

The only place indoors where you might use a ladder – or more likely one section of an extension ladder – is when you're painting the stairwell. You can stand the ladder on a tread, facing the opposite way to the stairs, to reach the walls above them. If you want the ladder facing the other way, nail a piece of scrap wood to the tread it's standing on to prevent it slipping as you climb it.

TRESTLES AND STAGING

If you're undertaking a full-scale make-over that's likely to take a while, it could be worth hiring some access equipment for the duration of the job. For example, if you're decorating a lot of ceilings, some aluminium trestles and a length of aluminium staging make a safe and stable work platform. You can get staging up to 7.2 m (24 ft) long – big enough to span the largest room and make a continuous walkway so that you can paper the ceiling without touching the ground.

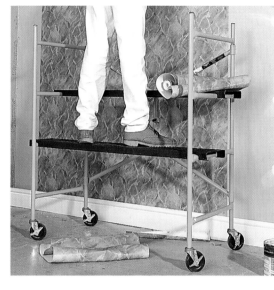

DECORATING STAIRWELLS

Papering the staircase really needs special access equipment. You'll find lash-ups using sections of

extension ladders, steps and scaffold boards illustrated in the best DIY books, but for my money I'd rather use something that's built for the job. It's back to the hire shop again, this time for a cunning contraption called a multi-purpose or combi ladder. This is a four-section, hinged ladder, which can be set up in several different ways so that you can reach all parts of the stairwell safely. It can be a straight ladder, a stepladder with unequal legs, or a flat work platform if used with a short section of staging as a deck. All the hinges lock in place automatically, and when set up, it's still narrow enough for people to squeeze past. Folded down, it's only 1 m (just over 3 ft) long and weighs a measly 12 kg (just under 28 lb), so you can take it home easily in the boot of your car.

preparing surfaces

As any professional decorator will tell you, preparation is the most important part of any job. Skimp on it and you'll never get good results. Do it properly, and you'll also make the job go more smoothly: paint will cover well, wallpaper will stick flat and tiles will stay put. Tackle the ceiling first, then the walls and finally the woodwork and any metalwork. Redecorate in the same order.

you will need

- Bucket, sponges and cloths
- Household detergent *or* sugar soap
- Long-handled sponge floor mop (for ceilings)
- Plaster filler and filling knife
- Fine glasspaper and sanding block

PREPARING WALLS AND CEILINGS

You can paint, paper or tile over existing painted surfaces. Old wallcoverings will have to come off (see page 70), unless they're the painted relief type and just need repainting. Tiles will have to come off too (see page 72) unless you want more tiles, in which case you can tile over them (see page 90).

1 Wash painted walls with a solution of detergent or sugar soap, working from the bottom upwards so that dirty water running down the wall doesn't leave difficult-to-shift streaks. Rinse with clean water and leave to dry.

2 Use a floor mop to wash ceilings – it's far less effort than doing the job by hand, but you'll have to use a damp cloth to wash around light fittings so that they don't get soaked. Take lampshades down first, and wrap other

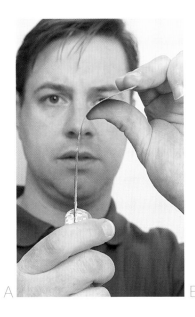

A

B

C

pendant lights in a big polythene bag so that they don't get splashed. Rinse the ceiling surface with clean water and leave it to dry.

3 Rake out any cracks with your filling knife – this has a bendy blade (A), whereas the similar-looking stripping knife has a stiff one – to remove loose material and give the filler a chance to stick.

4 Wedge in some filler (B), leaving it slightly proud of the surrounding surface so that it can be sanded flush when set hard.

5 Tackle deep holes by applying filler in layers (C), letting each one set before you add the next. If you try to fill deep holes in one go, the filler will simply slump out of the hole.

PREPARING WOODWORK

Most woodwork around the house will be either painted or varnished. If it is in good condition, you can redecorate it with the minimum of preparation. If it's chipped, full of cracks or has been painted many times over the years, the best bet is to strip the old finish off back to bare wood and start again from scratch (see page 68).

1 If the woodwork is in good condition, simply wet your sanding sponge and rub it over the surface to remove the shine and smooth off any bits that got stuck in the old paint or varnish. Rinse out the sponge when it gets clogged with paint.

2 If there are any chips in the paintwork, touch them in with some filler and sand them smooth when set.

3 Wash the surface with a solution of detergent or sugar soap. Rinse off with clean water and leave to dry, ready for repainting.

PREPARING TILES

If you're tiling over existing tiles, all you have to do is wash the surface with detergent or sugar soap to remove grease and dirt, rinse it with clean water and leave to dry. If any tiles are loose, prise them out and fill the space with plaster filler. Don't worry about repairing any loose or missing grouting. The next layer of tile adhesive will cover it.

lifesaver

Old houses might still have a type of paint called distemper on their ceilings. If it washes off like chalk on your mop, stop work and buy a can of stabilizing solution, a special primer for porous surfaces. Brush on two coats of this to seal the surface ready for repainting.

decorating and diy

you will need

- **Fine wet-and-dry sanding sponge**

- **General-purpose filler and filling knife**

- **Sandpaper**

- **Bucket, sponges and cloths**

- **Household detergent *or* sugar soap**

stripping paint

Nine times out of ten, it's straightforward to paint over existing paint on wood and metal surfaces around the house. But sometimes old paintwork can get badly chipped, or be so thick from previous redecoration that it's obscuring decorative detail or making doors and windows stick. There's only one solution: strip it all off and start again. Here's how to do it.

you will need

- Heat gun
- Stripping knife
- Container for stripper
- Paint stripper
- Paintbrush
- Combination shavehook
- Water *or* white spirit for neutralizing stripper
- Cloths
- Fine glasspaper
- Wood filler *or* coloured wood stopping
- Filler knife
- Wire wool

CHOOSE YOUR WEAPON

There are two ways of stripping paint from wood and metal. You can heat the paint film with a blast of hot air from a heat gun, or you can apply a liquid chemical stripper. Both methods soften the paint so that you can scrape it off with a metal stripping knife – or with a tool called a shavehook on fiddly mouldings. Which method you choose depends on what you're stripping and how you plan to redecorate it afterwards.

A heat gun (A) is best for large areas, or for surfaces you intend to repaint. (The heat can leave scorch marks on wood, which would show if you varnished the surface.) You also have to use the gun with care near glass. If it has a heat-shield attachment, fit this to the nozzle to stop the hot air overheating the glass and cracking it.

A chemical stripper (B) is best on surfaces with a lot of detail, or those you intend to varnish. It is also better than a heat gun for stripping paint from

A

B

metal, which conducts the heat away as fast as you apply it. Gel or paste-type strippers stay put better than liquid ones on vertical surfaces. With all strippers you have to neutralize their effect once the old paint has been removed in order to stop them attacking the new finish. Some brands need water for this, while others need white spirit; always check the instructions on the can.

Take care when using heat guns and chemical strippers. The former can burn if pointed carelessly and the scrapings are hot, so wear leather gloves. The latter can splash and sting skin and eyes, so wear PVC gloves and safety goggles for protection.

1 **For a large area**: play hot air from the heat gun over the surface you're stripping. Start scraping the paint off (A) as soon as it starts to bubble up, and deposit the scrapings in an old paint tin or similar heat-resistant container. Tackle mouldings first so that you don't char surrounding surfaces.

For a smaller area: with liquid or paste stripper, brush it on and leave it to blister the paint (B). Then scrape it off with a flat scraper (or a shavehook on mouldings), and dump the gooey mess in an old paint tin. Finish off by washing the surface down with water or white spirit, then sand it lightly with fine glasspaper. Paste strippers work best on surfaces such as metal fireplace surrounds, which would soak up heat from the hot-air gun and make stripping very hard work. Give the paste time to penetrate the layers of paint, then scrape it off bit by bit.

2 Once the surface is back to bare wood or metal, finish off by neutralizing the stripper as directed on the tin. Then sand wood smooth, filling any dents and splits with wood filler if you're repainting, and with coloured wood stopping if you're varnishing. Metal just needs a rub down with some wire wool.

WARNING

top tip

Use an old toothbrush to work paint stripper into awkward corners. If you're stripping old stained wood, use a pad of wire wool to scrub the stripper into the wood grain and lift the sticky stain right off. Wear PVC work-gloves to protect your hands.

stripping wall coverings

As a general rule, old wall coverings have to come off before you can redecorate. The trouble with painting or wallpapering over them is that any bits not stuck properly to the wall beneath will lift, causing unsightly bubbles. And if the existing wallpaper has a plastic surface, ordinary wallpaper paste simply won't stick to it anyway. So get ready to do some stripping.

lifesaver

In old houses you might come across a heavy-duty moulded wall covering called Lincrusta. This was often used up to dado rail height in halls and stairwells because of its durability, and will probably have several coats of paint on it. Use a perforator followed by a steam stripper to loosen the wall covering bit by bit. The steam will soften the special Lincrusta adhesive, enabling you to peel it off the wall covering gradually.

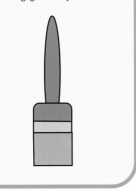

CHECK WHAT'S THERE

Before you start stripping your old wallpaper, do a simple test to find out what you're up against. First splash on some water. If it soaks in, you have an ordinary paper that will be simple to remove. If it doesn't soak in, try to lift a corner of the paper at a seam. If you can peel off a plastic surface layer easily, you have a vinyl wallpaper – again, easy to strip once you've removed the vinyl surface layer. If the surface won't peel off, you have a washable paper, and stripping this will be much harder work. So will stripping any wallpaper that's been painted over, such as woodchip or Anaglypta.

ORDINARY WALLPAPER

1 To strip ordinary wallpaper, all you have to do is wet it. The water can be applied either with a sponge, or with a small garden spray gun (A). The paper absorbs the water, which then softens the old paste, letting you scrape the whole lot off with your stripping knife. Scoring the surface with a serrated scraper or a proprietary wheeled perforator will help the water soak in more quickly.
2 Re-soak or spray any stubborn bits that don't come off first time.

A

WASHABLE OR PAINTED WALLPAPER

1 To strip a washable or painted wallpaper, you need a tool to perforate the surface coating (A) and a steam stripper that will force steam through the coating and into the paste beneath (B). Hire one for an occasional job, but it's better value to buy one if you have several rooms to strip. Fill the boiler of the steamer with hot tap water so it comes to the boil more quickly, plug it in and switch it on.

2 Meanwhile, use your perforating tool to make tiny holes in the surface coating.

3 When the steam stripper comes to the boil, hold the steaming plate against the wall over a seam for 10 or 15 seconds, then move it to the adjacent wall surface while you start to scrape and strip the steamed area. Carry on area by area until the wall is completely stripped. As you work, keep an eye on the water level in the stripper's reservoir. You'll need to top it up from time to time if you're stripping a whole room.

B

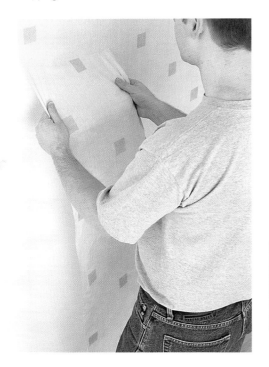

C

VINYL WALLPAPER

1 To strip a vinyl wallpaper, pick the corner away from the wall at the bottom of each length and peel off the vinyl surface layer (C). Working from bottom to top, it should come away in one continuous strip (no soaking is needed).

2 All you have to do then is soak and scrape off the porous backing layer, which will come off as easily as an ordinary paper. Don't be tempted to leave this on the wall if you're hanging more wallpaper; it may not be perfectly stuck, and it's sure to bubble up in places when it's soaked by the new paste.

top tip

Put down dustsheets before you start stripping wallpaper, and have some big rubbish bags handy so you can stuff the paper into them as you work, instead of treading sticky scraps all over the floor.

removing other decorations

A problem with lots of room make-overs is getting rid of the old decorations, especially if they were applied by previous owners and you don't have a clue how they did it. The main problems are polystyrene ceiling tiles, Artex-type textured coatings, timber wall cladding, cork and ceramic wall tiles and old floor coverings. Here's how to tackle each one.

A

TEXTURED COATINGS

How you get rid of these depends on what they are. The job will be slow and messy work, so clear the room of all furniture, put down lots of dust sheets and wear a pair of safety goggles, plus a cap of some sort if you're using a chemical stripper.

1 Artex and similar products are plaster-based, so soften and strip using a steam stripper (A).

2 Modern textured finishes are basically thickened emulsion paints, and generally have a lower relief effect than Artex. You can strip these with textured paint remover, a special type of paint stripper. If you can't face all this, have the ceiling replastered instead.

POLYSTYRENE CEILING TILES

These outdated cover-ups often conceal a poor ceiling, so be prepared for a lot of renovation work once you've removed them.

1 If the tiles were put up with adhesive blobs, prise them off, then tackle the blobs left behind. Although these should scrape off, you'll probably damage the plaster.

2 Get a plasterer to give the ceiling a new skim coat of plaster, or consider hiding the mess with a new textured finish.

If the tiles were stuck on with a continuous bed of adhesive, leave them be and have a new plasterboard ceiling installed to sandwich the tiles between it and the existing ceiling. Sounds like another job for the plasterer…

TIMBER WALL CLADDING

1 To remove tongued-and-grooved cladding, first prise off any edge trims. Then try to lever away the boards at each side of the wall, one of which will have had its tongue removed when it was fitted.
2 Once that's off, you can prise the rest from their supporting framework of timber battens one by one with an old chisel and a hammer. **3** Finish off by removing the wall battens and making good the fixing holes.

CORK WALL TILES

These will probably have been stuck on with contact adhesive, and therefore held really fast. Don't even think of trying to remove them. Instead, give them a coat of wallpaper size (diluted wallpaper paste), then hang lining paper over them, ready for painting or papering.

CERAMIC WALL TILES

1 You can hack ceramic tiles off the wall with a brick bolster and hammer, but this will wreck the surface underneath, which will need to be replastered if you want to paint or paper it.
2 If you decide to go ahead, start work at an edge or external corner, and work along the rows tile by tile (B) until you've hacked off the tiles and as much of the old adhesive as you can.

OLD FLOOR COVERINGS

In a nutshell, some can stay and some have to go. In the first category come vinyl and cork tiles that are well stuck down to the floor surface, and also sheet vinyl. If any of these have been laid over hardboard, however, it's a simple job to prise this up sheet by sheet, bringing the old floor covering with it.

Ceramic or quarry tiles can be covered with a thin layer of self-smoothing compound, a product that dries to a hard surface ready for a new floor covering to be laid on top. Old tiles can be tiled over if they're on a concrete floor, but not if they're on a timber one – it probably won't be able to take the extra weight.

Old carpet and its underlay should always be lifted and discarded. It's easy to pull it away from the gripper strips around the edge of the room (C), and the underlay will probably be loose-laid. It's a false economy to re-use old underlay beneath a brand new carpet, but there's no harm in reusing the gripper strips if they're secure.

B

top tip

If you want different ceramic tiles, you can simply stick new tiles on top of the old ones. Modern tile adhesives are well up to the job, and you'll save yourself a lot of hard work by taking this short cut, but you can do it only the once. Finish off the edges of half-tiled areas with wooden mouldings stuck in place with panel adhesive, or use ceramic tile edge trims stuck on a thicker-than-usual bed of adhesive.

C

painting walls and ceilings

After all that tedious preparation work (see pages 66–73), you can now get on with the rewarding part of the job – applying a fresh coat of paint to the walls and ceilings. You can do this with a brush, a roller or a pad – whatever you prefer – but it's worth trying them all if you haven't done any painting work before, to see which one you get on with best.

GETTING READY

Before starting work, make sure you have everything you need. If you've followed my advice, you'll have worked out how much paint you'll need (see page 62), and bought a bit extra. You'll also have the tools you require (see page 46), and you'll have given some thought to access equipment (see page 64) – steps, probably, although trestles and staging make light work of painting ceilings. Now it's time to put down the dust sheets and get started.

1 Dust the top of the paint container, then prise off the lid. Stir the paint if there's any clear liquid on the surface, and leave it to stand for an hour if

A   B

you will need

- Emulsion paint – choose matt or silk (see pages 40–1) according to the effect you want

- Stick or spoon for stirring

- Paint brushes – 75 or 100 mm (3 or 4 in) for the main areas and a 50 mm (2 in) one for touching in around the edges
  or
- Paint roller – the 230 mm (9 in) size puts paint on more quickly than the smaller 180 mm (7 in) size

- Roller sleeve – short pile for smooth surfaces, long pile for textured ones, such as Artex ceilings and woodchip or embossed wallpaper

- Roller tray
  or
- Paint pads – a large rectangular pad for the main areas and a smaller one for the edges

- Pad-loading tray

it's a non-drip type so that it can turn back into a jelly. Then set up your access equipment. If you're painting a whole room, do the ceiling first.

2 **If using a brush:** dip it into the paint to about half the bristle depth and scrape off any excess by wiping it against the inside edge of the container. Then start painting. Brush the paint on in parallel strips first, then brush across the strips in the same direction to blend them together. Finish off with light brush strokes in the original direction (A). Reload the brush and repeat the process, completing a strip of wall or ceiling about 300 mm (12 in) wide at a time before starting the next strip. On walls, start in the top right-hand corner if you're right-handed, and the left-hand corner if you're left-handed. On ceilings, start above the main window.

If using a roller: pour the paint into your roller tray to a depth of about 25 mm (1 in). Run the roller down the slope of the tray and into the paint, then roll it up and down the slope to load the sleeve evenly. Roll the paint on to the wall or ceiling in two or three parallel bands at a time, then work the roller across the area. Finish by rolling in the original direction (B and C). Reload the sleeve whenever it begins to run dry. You won't be able to paint right into internal corners with a roller; go as close as you can, then touch in the edge strips with a paintbrush.

If using paint pads: pour the about 12 mm (½ in) of paint into the loading tray. Hold the pad parallel to the surface of the paint and dip it in. Squeeze out excess paint on the slope of the tray. Start painting, drawing the pad over the surface in touching parallel bands. Then draw it lightly across the bands to blend them together and finish off with light strokes in the original direction. That's all there is to it. As with rollers, you might need to use a smaller pad or a paintbrush to touch in the edges of the area.

top tip

If you're planning to repaint your house from top to bottom, it might be worth considering one of two options to speed the work up. The first is to use a pressurised paint roller. This has a paint reservoir which feeds paint continuously into the roller sleeve, allowing you to carrying on painting without having to reload the sleeve at regular intervals. The second is to buy an airless spray gun. This electrically powered tool really puts paint on the walls quickly, but you have to be prepared to clear each room completely of furniture and also to mask off woodwork and any other surfaces before you start work.

C

painting wood and metal

Your home will contain quite a lot of woodwork – doors, windows, skirting boards, the staircase and so on – which will either need painting or, if it is attractive wood, varnishing (see page 78). The only metal surfaces you're likely to decorate are radiators and pipework. See pages 66–73 for preparing sufaces first.

you will need

- Dust sheets
- Masking tape
- Screwdriver for removing door and window fittings
- Screws for temporary handles
- Solvent-based paint – choose high gloss, satin gloss or eggshell, according to the finish you want
- Paint brushes – a 50 mm (2 in) brush for main areas and 12 and 25 mm (½ and 1 in) brushes for fiddly bits, such as window glazing bars
- Plastic or cardboard shield

PICKING THE RIGHT PAINT

It's usual to paint both wood and metal with a solvent-based paint, although there is a limited range of water-based paints for wood which can be used as an alternative if you don't like the smell of solvent evaporating as the paint dries. However, for recoating existing paintwork – your likeliest painting job – it's best to stick to the same paint type that's been used before, and this will almost certainly have been solvent-based. This means you can be sure that the new paint will be compatible with the old.

1 Spread out your dust sheets generously, taking them under the door frame. Prepare the doors by unscrewing and removing the door handles, and the hinged windows by removing the handles and stays and driving a wood screw into one of the screw holes on each opening section to act as a temporary handle.

2 Dust the top of the tin and prise off the lid. Dip your brush in to half the bristle length, wipe off the excess on the inside edge of the tin and start painting. Brush the paint on in bands parallel with the grain of the wood, then blend the strips together with strokes across the grain. Finish off with light strokes along it. Use a similar technique on radiators, applying vertical bands first. Let the radiators cool down first; if they're hot, the paint will dry too quickly and spoil the finish. On pipe work, brush around the pipe in bands, then smooth the paint out with light strokes along the line of the pipe.

3 Paint doors section by section, after wedging the door in the open position. Divide a flush door by eye into sections about half a door's width square and paint it section by section, starting at one top corner. On a panelled door,

A

B

C

paint the mouldings round each panel first, then fill in the panel (A). When you've painted all the panels, tackle the vertical parts between them, then the horizontal rails and finally the two long side sections, known as the stiles.

If the door faces are being painted in two different colours, paint the latch edge the same colour as the face that opens into the room, and the hinge edge to match the other face.

4 Paint hinged windows in sections too. Paint the opening sections first, after putting masking tape round the glass (B) then tackle the fixed frame and finish off with the window-sill (C). Replace the stays and their pegs as soon as you finish painting so that you can prop the window open while the paint dries.

To paint a sash window, push the inner sash half-way up and pull the outer sash all the way down. Paint the inner sash and the bottom part of the outer sash, plus the exposed parts of the side grooves in which the sashes slide. When the paint is touch-dry, reverse the sashes so that you can paint the upper part of the outer sash and the rest of the grooves. Finish off by painting the rest of the frame and the window-sill.

5 When painting skirting boards, use a plastic or cardboard paint shield to keep the paint off the floor covering. Place it into the gap between the skirting board and the floor, then paint that section of board. Wipe it clean of paint, move it along to the next section and repeat the process.

above **Reverse the sashes and paint the lower part of the outer sash.**

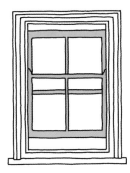

above **Paint the top of the outer sash, then the inner one.**

above **Finish off by painting the vertical beads and the frame.**

using varnish and wood stains

If you want the grain and natural colour of your woodwork to be visible, a clear varnish is the perfect finish. And if you want to change its colour too – either to that of a different wood, or to a bright colour – you can stain it first, or else use a coloured varnish if you want to do both the colouring and the finishing in one go.

you will need

- Wet-and-dry sanding sponge
- Clean, lint-free cloth (old handkerchiefs are ideal)
- White spirit
- Paintbrush
- Clear or coloured varnish
- Fine glasspaper
- Wood stain
- Container for wood stain

lifesaver

If you end up with a stained shade you hate, don't panic. Buy a wood bleach and follow the instructions; this will get the wood back almost to the colour you started with. If you've varnished over the stain, strip the coating with varnish remover first.

OLD WORK OR NEW

A varnished wooden surface shows everyday wear and tear less than a painted one, but it will eventually need a fresh coat of varnish to keep it looking good. If you want a change of appearance, try using a coloured varnish. If you want to use stain and varnish on wood that's been painted, you must first strip off the old paint with a chemical paint stripper. On new wood, you have complete freedom of choice – plain varnish, coloured varnish, or, if you want real depth of colour, wood stain followed by a clear varnish for extra durability.

ON EXISTING VARNISHED WOODWORK

1 Key the surface ready for the new varnish by sanding it lightly with the finest surface of your sanding sponge. Then wipe the surface over with a cloth moistened with white spirit to remove any dust, dirt and grease.
2 Brush on a coat of new varnish, just as if you were painting, brushing first along the grain (A), then across it and finally along the grain again.
3 On curved surfaces, such as chair legs, brush around the curve first, then draw the brush lightly along the grain direction.

ON STRIPPED WOODWORK AND ON NEW WOOD

1 Sand the surface smooth with fine glasspaper and dust it off with a cloth moistened with white spirit.
2 If you are just varnishing it, add one part of white spirit to nine parts of varnish and apply this as the first sealing coat, using a cloth pad rather than a brush. This diluted mixture penetrates the surface and bonds to the wood better than neat varnish.

A

3 Sand the surface lightly when it's dry, then apply two full-strength coats of varnish, again sanding lightly between coats.

IF USING A WOOD STAIN

1 Always apply a little to an unseen part of the wood first to test the depth of colour. You can dilute stains (with water or white spirit – check the can for details) to get a paler colour, and you can mix stains of the same solvent type to get darker or intermediate shades.

2 Apply the stain with a cloth pad rather than a brush, working along the grain of the wood in parallel but not overlapping bands – overlaps show up as a darker shade.

3 Sand the surface very lightly when it's dry to remove any raised wood fibres, dust it and apply a second coat of stain if you want a deeper shade still.

4 Finish off with two coats of neat varnish applied with a brush, to give the stained wood a durable and waterproof finish.

cleaning painting equipment

There are two schools of thought about cleaning up at the end of a painting job. One says buy cheap brushes, roller sleeves and paint pads, and bin the lot when you've finished. The other says buy good-quality stuff and look after it. As you get better results with better tools, I'm in the second school...and anyway, good brushes actually get better the more you use them. You bin if you want to.

you will need

- Old newspapers
- Lots of tap water
- Nylon scourer
- Kitchen paper
- White spirit
- Container for soaking brushes – clean glass jars are ideal
- Washing-up liquid
- Kitchen foil and clear food wrap
- Plastic shopping bags

USING SOLVENTS

Getting solvent-based paint out of brushes usually means using a solvent called white spirit. This isn't very pleasant to use – many people hate the smell, and it's not very kind to skin either – so, if possible, do your cleaning up outdoors, and wear rubber gloves when handling spirit-soaked brushes.

When you've finished cleaning your brushes, don't pour the used solvent down the drain. Keep it in a jam jar or a glass bottle and leave it to settle for a few days. Then you can pour off the almost clear liquid for re-use, leaving just the paint sludge in the jar. Stuff in some kitchen paper to soak this up, screw the top back on and put it in the dustbin.

A

B

lifesaver

If white spirit won't clean a brush that's really clogged with half-dried paint, stand it in a jar of proprietary brush cleaner or even paint stripper overnight. Then try cleaning it in hot soapy water the next morning. If the paint has dried rock hard and it's your favourite brush, use a wire brush to get the worst of the paint out of the bristles before dunking it in the cleaner overnight. It should clean up a treat in the morning if you wash it with white spirit and follow up with hot soapy water as before.

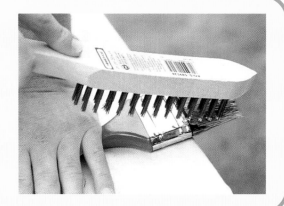

1 When you finish painting, always squeeze as much paint as you can out of whatever tool you've been using by working it backwards and forwards on sheets of newspaper. There's no point in having to remove more paint than necessary. Fold up the paint-soaked paper and bin it.

2 **If you've been using a plastic roller and paint pad trays,** scrub out with clean water, using a nylon pan scourer to get rid of the dried-on bits.

If you've been using paint pads, they are the easiest tool to clean, because they hold less paint than brushes and rollers. Run tap water into the pile, squeeze it against the sink from time to time, then leave it to dry when it's clean.

If you've been using a brush with solvent-based paint, pour enough white spirit or brush cleaner into a glass jar or paint kettle (A) to take the full depth of the bristles. Work them up and down in the liquid to dissolve as much of the paint as possible. Then take the brush to the sink and wash it in hot soapy water to get rid of the spirit. Wrap it in kitchen paper and leave to dry. This makes sure the bristles keep their shape as they dry – you'll end up with useless flyaway bristles if you leave them out to dry in the open air.

If you've been brushing with emulsion paint, head for the kitchen sink. Hold the brush bristle-end up under running water, occasionally stopping to flex the bristles backwards and forwards against the bottom of the sink and squeeze out more paint. When the water running from the brush becomes clear, it's clean. Shake out the excess water, wrap the bristles in kitchen paper so that they keep their shape, and leave the brush to dry.

If you've been using a roller, run tap water over the sleeve. Roll it up and down the slope of the roller tray, squeezing until no more watery paint flows out (B). Remove the sleeve from the roller and leave to dry, then store it in a plastic bag.

top tip

Whenever you stop work for any length of time during a painting job, wrap your brush or paint pad in some kitchen foil or clear food-wrap. This stops the paint from drying and keeps the tool workable for when you restart. If using a roller, wrap it in a plastic bag and squeeze the air out, and put the paint tray in a plastic carrier bag and tie the handles together.

papering walls 1

Paper-hanging is one of those jobs you either love or hate, but getting the hang of it yourself will save you a big decorator's bill and let you give your home a facelift whenever you want. Papering is a really satisfying job because it transforms a room far more dramatically than paint.

STRAIGHT AND TRUE

The three most important words in the paper-hanger's vocabulary are vertical, vertical and vertical. Every time you turn a corner, mark a plumbed line on the next wall and hang the next length alongside it so that you know it's vertical, which room corners often aren't. Remember that and you can't go wrong (well, not *far* wrong! – see pages 84–5).

For your first attempt, try hanging plain lining paper: there's no pattern to match up, it will provide the ideal backing for some proper wallpaper and you can strip it all off again easily if you make a real mess of things. Alternatively, use a tough vinyl without a pattern match if you're more confident of your untried paper-hanging talents.

you will need

- Tape measure
- Pencil
- Plumb bob and string line – cheaper and more accurate than a spirit level, but use a level if you have one already
- Steps (don't try to balance on a chair: you'll fall off sooner or later)
- Lining paper
- Paper-hanging scissors
- Trimming knife
- Steel ruler
- Pasting table – hardboard ones cost only a few pounds
- Wallpaper paste, plus a bucket to mix it in and a clean wide paintbrush to apply it
- Paper-hanging brush (a sponge will do if you're hanging vinyl)

1 If your room has a chimney breast, find its centre and draw a vertical pencil line there (A). The strips will be centred neatly on the room's dominant feature – especially important if your paper is patterned rather than plain. If there is no chimney breast, start in a corner and draw your plumb line about 20 mm (¾ in) less than the width of the wallpaper away from it. This means you will be able to fold a small strip of the paper on to the adjacent wall to hide any gaps.

2 Measure the wall height and cut a strip of paper to length with your knife (B), adding about 100 mm (4 in) to allow for trimming at top and bottom.

A

B

C

D

3 Put the length of paper face down on your pasting table, aligning one end and the near edge with the table-top. Brush paste up the middle of the length and out towards the end and the near edge. Slide the paper over so it's now aligned with the far side, and paste out to that edge too (C). Fold the pasted part over on itself, then slide it along the table so that you can repeat the sequence to paste the rest.

4 Carry the folded paper to the wall, climb your steps and let the folds open out. Hold the top against the wall with about 50 mm (2 in) lapping on to the ceiling, and slide the paper across to the pencil line (D). When it's lined up, use your paper-hanging brush to smooth the paper into place, working down the centre first and then out towards the edges to get rid of any air bubbles. Crease the paper into the angles between the wall, ceiling and skirting board, then peel the paper back and trim it along the creases. Brush the trimmed ends back into place.

5 Repeat the process to hang subsequent lengths of paper, forming a neat butt join between them and trimming the top and bottom as before. Run a seam roller over the joins to ensure that they're well stuck down. Take care to match the pattern if the paper has one. This may be a straight edge-to-edge pattern, or may be offset by half the pattern repeat on opposite edges of the paper.

Turn the page to find out how to cope with corners, and how to hang paper around doors and windows.

top tip

Don't panic if you get bubbles in your freshly hung paper. The vast majority will disappear as the paper dries overnight. Any that remain have probably missed out on being pasted. Make two cuts at right angles across the bubble with a sharp knife, fold back the paper tongues formed, and brush a little paste on to the wall. Then smooth the tongues back in place.

papering walls 2

Now you've mastered the basics of paper-hanging, it's time to face the tricky bits – turning corners, hanging paper neatly around door and window openings, and trimming it to fit round the inevitable light switches and power points. None of these is difficult if you know how to tackle them properly.

FINISHING TOUCHES

As I mentioned on page 82, keeping the lengths truly vertical is the key to successful paper-hanging, but room corners often aren't true. This means that the edge of the length that turns the corner is hardly ever vertical, and if you hung another length next to it, that wouldn't be vertical either. The result? Patterns running gradually uphill or downhill instead of straight across the wall, and a complete mismatch as you eventually get back to your starting point. The solution is to turn only narrow strips of paper around corners, and to hang the rest of the strip on the next wall to a true plumbed line. Then you'll always stay on the straight and narrow.

1 When you reach an internal corner, measure the distance to it from the edge of the last full length. Cut a strip of paper to this width plus about 20 mm (¾ in), paste it and hang it. Brush the paper into the angle so that the 20 mm (¾ in) strip turns the corner. Make horizontal 'release' cuts into it if it won't lie flat – a sure sign that the corner isn't true.

2 Measure the width of the strip that you cut off from the length you've just hung and subtract 12 mm (½ in) from the measurement. Mark a plumbed line on the next wall, this distance away from the corner. Paste and hang the strip with its outer edge along the pencil line; its cut edge should just overlap the edge that turned the corner.

lifesaver

When hanging a length that needs a lot of trimming to fit, the edges of the paper can dry out and begin to curl away from the wall. Keep a paintbrush and a mug of mixed-up paste handy, so you can quickly brush a little extra paste on to the wall beneath the seams and get them to stick down firmly.

A

B

3 At external corners, cut a strip about 50 mm (2 in) wider than the distance to the corner, hang it and brush the overlap strip around the angle (A). Make horizontal release cuts if necessary so it lies flat. Mark a plumbed line on the next wall, the width of the offcut less 12 mm (½ in) away from the corner. Paste and hang the paper so its cut edge overlaps the turned edge. Use overlap adhesive to stick washables and vinyls.

4 When you reach a door, press the paper against the architrave (its wooden surround) and make a diagonal cut to the crease from the free edge of the length (B). Brush the paper into the angles between wall and architrave, mark it by running the blunt edge of your scissors along it, then peel it away so that you can trim off the waste. Brush the trimmed paper back into place. Repeat the process when you reach the other side of the frame.

5 Papering around windows looks tricky because there doesn't seem to be enough paper to go round. The secret is in the two little patches marked 8 and 9 in the diagram. These fill in the missing bits in the top corners after you've covered the sides of the recess.

6 If the paper lies over a light switch or power point, turn off the electricity at the mains. Then press the paper against the faceplate to reveal its outline, lift it away and pierce a hole in the centre. Make a diagonal cut from the hole to just beyond each corner mark, and cut off all but about 10 mm (⅜ in) of each flap. Unscrew the faceplate a little (C) so you can tuck the flaps behind it. Then tighten the screws and turn the electricity back on.

top tip

If you're hanging a washable or vinyl wallpaper, you need a tube of overlap adhesive to stick any overlaps. Peel back the top layer and apply a thin bead of adhesive down the edge of the paper underneath. Then brush the overlap back into place.

At recessed windows, hang the last complete length to one side of the opening (length 2) and trim to cover the side of the reveal. Paper above and below the window, repeating the trimming at the other side (7). Then fill in the patches (8 and 9 – see detail). To finish papering the underside of the reveal, cut matching patches and stick them in place so that they just turn on the wall. Peel back the last complete length and brush it over the patch.

papering ceilings and stairwells

Now that you've climbed the foothills of paper-hanging, it's time to tackle the Alps. Your final challenges are to paper a ceiling and the stairwell – both jobs that involve handling long lengths of pasted paper and needing good access equipment. Here's how to go about them.

you will need

- Access equipment
- Tools as required to remove light fittings
- Tape measure
- String line and chalk
- An extra pair of hands
- Wallpaper and paste
- Paper-hanging tools (see page 82)

top tip

When you come to a ceiling rose, pierce the paper and make several short scissor cuts radiating from it so that you can pull the pendant flex through the hole. Undo the ceiling rose cover and let it fall down the flex. Brush the triangular tongues of paper up to the rose baseplate, trim them to fit one by one, then screw the cover back on. Hang the rest of the length in the usual way (C).

PAPERING A CEILING

Once you get the hang of working upside-down (so to speak), papering a ceiling is easier than working on walls because ceilings have virtually no obstacles, apart from light fittings. The secret of success is to set up a proper work platform, such as trestles and staging (see page 64), so that you can walk the width of the room without stepping up and down. And it's definitely a job where having someone to help will come in very useful.

1 To make life easier, hang the ceiling paper across the narrower dimension of the room. With butt joints, it's no longer necessary to follow the old rule of papering parallel to the main window in order to avoid shadows at the joints. Set up your access equipment, and take down lampshades and light fittings.

2 Measure the width of the paper you're hanging. Then use your string line and your helper to mark a chalked line across the room about 25 mm (1 in) less than this width away from the wall where you plan to begin papering, so you're starting from the side of the room.

3 Measure the distance across the room and add 100 mm (4 in) to allow for trimming at the ends. Cut and paste the paper, folding it concertina fashion into a neat pile, then head for the ceiling.

4 With your helper behind you supporting the paper, take one end and offer it up into the wall/ceiling angle, aligning its long edge with the chalked line and letting about 50 mm (2 in) lap on to the end wall (A). Brush it into the angle and trim the end to fit. Work your way back across the room,

A   B   C

brushing the paper into place as you go. When you reach the far side, brush the paper into the angle and trim it. Finally, brush the long edge into the wall/ceiling angle, peel it away again and trim it to fit the side wall.

5 Hang subsequent lengths so that they butt against the edge of the previous length, trimming their ends as before (B). When you reach the other side of the room, cut a strip of paper about 25 mm (1 in) wider than the gap that's left to be papered, and hang and trim it as you did the first length.

PAPERING A STAIRWELL

It can be tricky matching patterns with the long lengths of paper needed on a stairwell, since they can stretch under their own weight as you hang them. For this reason, it's best to pick a strong paper with no pattern to match up. A vinyl wallpaper, which will stand up to the inevitable wear and tear of life on the stairs, is probably your best choice.

1 Having drawn a plumb line, start hanging the longest lengths first (see diagram), with a helper to support the folded paper while you align and brush it into position.

2 With subsequent lengths, work up towards the landing, then down to the hall. When measuring for the lengths that go on the stairs, take the measurement for the next length from the edge of the previous one you hung as you work your way up. Otherwise you'll be cutting lengths that turn out to be too short.

using borders and friezes

Borders and friezes are narrow strips of wallpaper that can be used in all sorts of ways to add a splash of colour to walls and even ceilings. Strictly speaking, borders frame things, such as doorways or groups of pictures, while friezes run around the room at ceiling height, or next to picture rails, dado rails and even skirting boards. However, most people refer to both things as borders nowadays.

you will need

- Pencil
- Spirit level
- Steel ruler
- Border
- Scissors
- Border adhesive
- Paper-hanging tools (see page 82)
- Trimming knife

top tip

If you plan to put up a border or two, experiment with the effect first by sticking strips to the walls with masking tape or poster putty. Then you can move them easily into a variety of positions and work out which looks best before you start hanging them for real.

PASTED OR STICKY?

Some borders have to be pasted just like wallpaper – fine if you're sticking them to emulsion walls or ordinary wallpaper, but not so good on washable or vinyl surfaces because ordinary wallpaper paste won't stick to them. Instead, you need to use special ready-mixed border adhesive, which comes in a tub, or pick a self-adhesive border in the first place. Paper types are low-tack and easy to hang, but peel-and-stick plastic ones with a release paper backing need handling with care because they stick instantly, and although you can (with care) peel off a misaligned section, you risk lifting the paint or wallpaper you're sticking it to.

1 Once you've decided where you want your border to go, draw light pencil guidelines on the wall to help you position it accurately. Use a spirit level and steel ruler or a long timber straightedge to mark a continuous horizontal guideline for a round-the-room border, unless you will be putting it next to the ceiling or a moulding such as a dado rail, in which case that will act as the guideline. Make sure lines for framing borders meet precisely at right angles.

2 Borders usually come in rolls 5 m (16 ft) long, so you shouldn't have too many joins. Cut lengths to match the wall or panel dimensions plus an allowance for trimming. Apply some paste if it's required and fold the length up concertina fashion. With self-adhesive borders, peel off a short length of the backing paper.

3 For a round-the-room border, position one end of the border in a room corner, against your pencil guideline, and start brushing it into place across the wall (A). Peel the backing paper off a self-adhesive border a little at a time, so that there's no risk of it sticking itself to the wall where it shouldn't. For a frame border, position the first length on its guideline with one end projecting just beyond and at right angles to it. Fix the next length so that it overlaps the first one by roughly the same amount, ready for trimming.

4 To butt-join lengths of border, stick the end of the second length over the end of the first one and match the pattern. Then cut through both layers using a sharp knife and your ruler, peel away the offcut of the second length and open up the joint so you can remove the offcut from the first length (B). Brush the cut ends back on to the wall.

5 When you get back to your starting-point, turn the last length around the final corner. Make an unobtrusive butt joint by cutting through both layers where they overlap, close to the corner on the first wall. Any pattern discontinuity won't be noticed here.

6 To form neat mitred corner joints where borders form a frame, hold your ruler at 45 degrees across the corner and cut through both layers of border with your knife (C). Peel away the offcuts and smooth the border back into place.

top tip

Borders are surprisingly expensive – the price of a 5 m (16 ft) long roll can often be much the same as for a standard 10.05 m (33 ft) roll of wallpaper. An economical way round this problem is to pick wallpaper or vinyl with a vertical design that can be cut down into border-sized strips with a trimming knife and straight edge on your pasting table. That way you'll get a whole lot of border for your money!

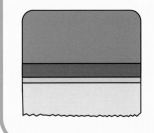

decorating and diy

A

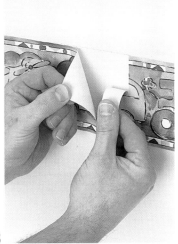

B

C

tiling walls

Ceramic tiles are the perfect choice when you want a wall surface that's tough, waterproof and easy to clean. You can tile just a small area such as a splashback in the kitchen, or tile an entire room. Whatever you decide, the basic principles are the same. See Preparing Surfaces, pages 66–73 first.

you will need

- Tiles
- Tiling gauge (home-made)
- All-in-one tile adhesive and grout
- Adhesive spreader
- Tile spacers
- Tape measure
- Pencil
- Tile-cutting jig
- Silicone sealant and cartridge gun
- Masking tape
- Damp cloth

PLANNING THE LAYOUT

The secret of success with tiles is to plan the layout carefully. Tiles look best if they're laid out symmetrically (i.e. centred) on the wall. If you're putting a few tiles behind a washbasin, for example, this is easy. You simply have to work out how many whole tiles to fit across the area, and then decide how many rows of tiles to put up. But if you're tiling wall to wall, you'll almost certainly have to cut tiles to complete the rows, and centring the layout means having to cut tiles of equal width at each end of the rows.

The best way of working out where to start tiling on a wall is to mark the mid-point and use a home-made tool called a tiling gauge to check how the tiles you've chosen will fit on the wall. Lay out a row of tiles on the floor, with small plastic tile spacers between them to ensure even spacings. Then place a length of wood alongside the row and mark the tile positions on it in pencil. Now you can hold this gauge against the wall with one end aligned with the wall's mid-point and see how big a gap will be left at the ends of each row. If the gap is very narrow (less than about 25 mm/1 in) or is almost a whole tile, it will be difficult to cut the tiles to fit. The way round this is to move the start point along from the mid-point by half a tile width; get the best compromise you can.

1 To tile a small area, such as a sink splashback, start by loose-laying the tiles on the kitchen worktop or floor so that, if you're using a mixture of colours, you can plan the layout (A). Then use your tiling gauge to find the right starting point.

A

B

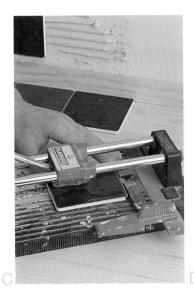
C

D

E

2 Spread enough adhesive on the wall to fix about half a dozen tiles. Hold the notched spreader almost at right angles to the wall so that it leaves neat ridges of adhesive. These squash down flat when the tiles are pressed into place. As you position each tile, place a tile spacer at each corner to keep the spacing even (B). Bed them well into the adhesive. Then the grout will cover them later.

3 You'll probably have to fit cut tiles at the ends of the rows. Measure the gap, allowing for the thickness of the tile spacers, and mark this on a tile. Then score and snap the tile using a proprietary cutting jig (C) – much more accurate than using a pencil-type cutter and a ruler, especially for small, thick tiles like the ones being used here.

4 When all the whole and cut tiles are in place, use the straight edge of the plastic spreader to fill the gaps (D). Either use an all-in-one adhesive and grout for this, or buy grout separately – essential if you want a coloured effect. Scrape off the excess grout as you work and leave to dry.

5 Use silicone mastic to make the join between splashback and worktop waterproof. Stick masking tape to both surfaces to leave a gap about 5 mm (¼ in) wide, then squeeze out the mastic along the line. Smooth off any lumps with a moistened finger, and peel off the tape when the mastic has developed a skin (E). Finish the job by wiping off smears of grout with a damp cloth.

TILING AROUND CORNERS

When tiling round an internal corner, set out the rows on each wall independently so that cut tiles meet in the angle. Leave an expansion gap where they meet. On walls with external corners, always start tiling each wall with a whole tile placed on the external angle.

TILING AROUND WINDOWS

Always centre tiling on a window recess, irrespective of whether it is itself centred on the wall. Tile the wall first, if possible with a row of whole tiles immediately below the recess. Then place whole tiles along the front edge of the recess, overlapping those on the wall, and fill in with cut tiles between these and the window frame.

cladding walls

Tongue-and-groove timber cladding has long been a popular way of giving walls a hard-wearing finish, especially in heavy traffic areas, such as hallways, and it's also an excellent cover-up for old plaster. However, it's quite expensive and takes a long time to fit plank by plank. You can achieve the same effect for a fraction of the price and in far less time by making your own panelling from MDF (medium-density fibreboard). All you need is a router...

you will need

- Tape measure
- Pencil
- 12 mm (½ in) MDF
- Handsaw *or* jigsaw
- 50 x 25 mm (2 x 1 in) wood for cutting guide and shelf
- Router with V-shaped cutter
- Two clamps
- Panel adhesive
- Architrave moulding
- Panel pins
- Power drill with 3 mm (⅛ in) twist drill bit and screwdriver bit
- 40 mm (1½ in) wood screws

top tip

Panel adhesive sticks for keeps. If you do want to remove the panelling when the room gets its next make-over, fix the panels and mouldings with screws driven into wallplugs.

USING A ROUTER

The router is one of the most versatile power tools. It's basically a high-speed drill with a flat, open baseplate through which steel cutters project. The cutters shape the surface the router is running across. Depending on what cutter is fitted, it can give a moulded edge to a piece of wood, or cut grooves with various profiles across its centre. For this project, it is set up to cut V-shaped grooves across a sheet of MDF and simulate the look of real tongue-and-groove cladding.

1 Decide how high you want your panelling to be and cut enough MDF panels to fit the wall. Lay them in a line next to each other on the floor and use a tape measure and a length of timber as a ruler to mark a series of parallel lines on the boards about 150 mm (6 in) apart (A). These are the positions of the grooves you're going to cut with the router.

2 Set the router up to cut grooves about 6 mm (¼ in) deep, and test the cutting depth on an MDF offcut. Then clamp a length of timber across the first MDF panel and use it to guide the edge of the router baseplate as you move it across the board. Set it half the width of the router baseplate away from the first

A

B

C

D

groove, and check that the cutter is exactly over the marked line. Start the router motor and run the cutter across the board in one steady movement. Reposition the timber guide for the next groove along and cut as before. Repeat the process to cut the rest of the grooves, then do the other boards.

3 Squirt squiggles of panel adhesive on to the back of an MDF panel (B). Rest its bottom edge on top of the skirting board and bring it up to the vertical, pressing it firmly into place against the wall. Repeat until all the panels are fixed in place.

4 Finish off the cladding with a shallow shelf and some decorative architrave moulding. Cut the wood for the shelf to length and hold it in place on top of the MDF so that you can mark a pencil line on the wall along its top edge.

5 Cut the architrave moulding to length and use more panel adhesive to stick it to the wall with its lower edge precisely on the pencil line. Tap in some panel pins at intervals to stop it slipping down the wall while the adhesive sets (C).

6 Slot the rear edge of the shelf into the gap between the MDF and the architrave. Secure it by drilling pilot holes every 300 mm (12 in) up through its underside at an angle and then driving in the 40 mm (1½ in) screws (D). Prime and paint everything to finish the job (E).

E

laying floor tiles

The big advantage of floor tiles is that they're small, manageable and easier to fit round obstacles than any sheet floor covering. That's why cork, vinyl and lino tiles are so popular for rooms, such as bathrooms, which are full of obstacles. But there's nothing to stop them being used anywhere in the house where you want a floor covering that's good-looking, hard-wearing and easy to keep clean.

you will need

- Tiles
- Hardboard for underlay
- Coppered hardboard pins
- Hammer
- Nail punch
- Tape measure
- Pencil
- String and drawing pins
- Handsaw *or* jigsaw
- Paper for template
- Trimming knife

top tip

If your cutting isn't too good and you've got gaps at the edges, hide them by pinning lengths of slim quadrant beading to the skirting boards all round the room. Prime and paint them first so that you don't risk getting paint on your brand new floor.

CHOOSING YOUR TILES

Most 'soft' floor tiles are sold with a self-adhesive backing, which makes laying them quick and simple; the only tool you need is a sharp knife for cutting and trimming them to fit around the edge of the room. With self-adhesive tiles, you can use the floor as soon as you've finished laying it. Cork tiles are available in two versions – PVC-coated with self-adhesive backing, or plain. If you want to save money, buy plain tiles (which you have to stick down with flooring adhesive) and seal them yourself with three or four coats of varnish. Of course, this takes time, and you can't use the floor until you've finished the job, so perhaps self-adhesive tiles are best, even if they do cost more.

1 You can tile straight onto chipboard or smooth concrete floors. If your floor is boarded, however, the board edges will show through the tiles. The solution is to cover the boards with a hardboard overlay, pinned to them with special coppered hardboard pins which don't rust. Drive them in at 150 mm (6 in) intervals right across each board (A) to ensure that it can't lift – a tedious but necessary job.

2 Next, find the mid-points of the walls and pin lengths of string between opposite walls. They will cross at the centre of the room, which is where you start tiling. If you start at one edge of the room, you will have some very awkward pieces to cut at

A

B

C

D

the other edges because rooms are seldom truly square. Mark pencil guidelines on the floor and remove the strings. Peel off the backing paper from the first tile and position it in the right angle where the lines meet (B).

3 Continue laying tiles out from the centre towards the walls, working on one quarter of the floor at a time. When you've laid all the whole tiles, cut the edge tiles with your knife. To do this accurately, don't measure each one. Instead place a tile on top of the last whole tile near the skirting board, and put another one on top of this with its edge pressed against the skirting board. Mark a line on the middle tile along the outer edge of the top tile, and cut the middle tile along this line. The part of the middle tile that was exposed in the three-tile 'sandwich' will fit the edge gap exactly.

4 At doorways, use a pencil and a piece of paper the same size as the tiles to trace off the profile of the door architrave (C). Cut along the pencil line with your trimming knife (D), then use the shaped edge of the paper to transfer the profile on to the tile.

5 Use the same technique to take the profile of any other obstacles you come up against. Then cut the tile carefully to shape with your knife, peel off the backing paper and stick the tile into place.

laying woodstrip flooring

There's no doubt that woodstrip flooring has knocked carpet off its perch as the must-have flooring in many people's homes. It's smart, warm under foot, hard-wearing and much easier to keep clean than carpet, which harbours the dust and house mites responsible for causing so many allergies nowadays. Best of all, it's easy to lay yourself.

PAYING FOR QUALITY

Woodstrip flooring is a laminate, rather like plywood, but with layers of different thicknesses. The thick baseboard gives the material its strength, while the wood surface you see on the top is either a real wood veneer or a printed plastic imitation. The whole lot is usually topped off by a clear wear layer, which also seals the surface of real wood types. These are the most expensive, but they're also the hardest-wearing.

The flooring comes in planks that are usually about 1.2 m (about 4 ft) long and 300 mm (12 in) or so wide. They have tongued-and-grooved edges, so each interlocks with its neighbours to form a continuous floor surface that literally floats on top of the existing floor. Most brands of plank are glued together; one or two others are held together by metal clips that fit in grooves in the underside of the planks.

1 On uneven timber floors, it's best to put down a plywood overlay first to create a perfectly flat, stable surface. Measure, mark with a pencil and cut the boards to size as necessary, and fix them with screws driven in at 150 mm (6 in) intervals (A). Then put down the

you will need

- 6 mm (¼ in) plywood overlay
- Tape measure
- Pencil
- 18 mm (¾ in) wood screws
- Flooring underlay and adhesive tape
- Heavy-duty polythene (for concrete floors)
- Packs of flooring
- Perimeter wedges
- PVA wood adhesive or fixing clips
- Handsaw or jigsaw
- Hammer
- Tamping block (optional)
- Edge beading and panel pins
- Mitre box and tenon saw

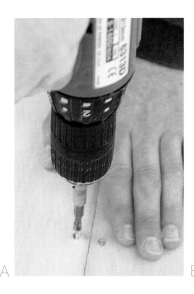

A

B

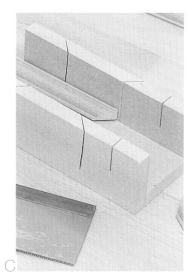

C

flooring underlay, which cushions the new flooring, and tape the joints between the lengths. On concrete floors, put down heavy-duty polythene first to guard against any risk of damp.

2 Start laying the first row of planks with their grooved edges facing the wall. Place perimeter wedges between them and the skirting boards at roughly 600 mm (2 ft) intervals to provide an expansion gap. Squirt some PVA adhesive into the grooved end of each board, and slot it over the tongue of the one you've just laid. If there's a radiator on the wall, cut a notch in the plank to fit round it (B). Cut the last plank in the row to length, including an allowance for the perimeter wedge, and glue it to its neighbour.

3 Use the offcut from the first row to start the next one, then carry on adding whole planks as outlined in srep 2 to complete the second row. Don't forget to fit a perimeter wedge at the end of the row. Glue all the joints, and use the hammer and the tamping block or a plank offcut – needed to protect the fragile tongued edges – to close them up fully as you lay each plank.

4 Continue working across the room in this way until you have just the last row of planks to lay. These will almost certainly need cutting down in width. Measure the width of the strip needed, including an allowance for the perimeter wedges, and cut the strips with a jigsaw. Then glue their edges and ends and slot them into position one by one to complete the floor. Now you can remove all the perimeter wedges, leaving just the expansion gap to fill.

5 Cut and pin lengths of quarter-circle (quadrant) beading to the skirting board to conceal the expansion gap. Use a mitre box and tenon saw to cut neat corner mitres (C). It's a good idea to varnish the beading before you fit it.

top tip

Unwrap the planks and store them in the room where they will be laid for at least 48 hours before you start work. This allows them to acclimatize to the room temperature and humidity, and prevents them from expanding and bowing upwards when they've been laid.

laying sheet vinyl

When you want a floor covering that's completely waterproof and easy to keep clean, sheet vinyl is the stuff to go for. Since it comes in rolls up to 4m (13 ft) wide, you get a seamless floor covering in all but the largest rooms. It's available in a wide range of designs and colourways to suit your décor and the cushioned types are warm under foot.

you will need

- Brown paper or newspaper for template
- Adhesive tape
- Scribing block, felt-tip pen and china marker
- Sheet vinyl
- Trimming knife
- Steel ruler
- Double-sided flooring tape

top tip

Sheet vinyl is more supple and easier to handle when it's warm. The day before you want to lay it, unroll it and leave it to acclimatize to room temperature.

DIFFERENT TECHNIQUES

In a normal-sized room with few obstacles at floor level, such as a kitchen, dining room or children's nursery, you can roll out sheet vinyl like a carpet. Cut it a little oversize and let the excess lap up the walls. Cut across the corners of the sheet at an angle of 45 degrees so that they will lie flat in the room corners. Then press the edges down into the angle between the the skirting board and floor, and trim off the excess with a sharp knife. Finally, use double-sided adhesive tape to stick the edges of the sheet down all round the room. Stick down any seams between lengths in large rooms in the same way.

In bathrooms and WCs, this method simply won't work because you have no room to manoeuvre the sheet and there are too many obstacles on the floor. The answer is to make a paper template of the floor, and use this to cut the sheet into a perfectly matched fit. Here's how it works.

1 Tape sheets of paper together to form a template that reaches to within 25 mm (1 in) of the room perimeter. Tear it to fit closely round obstacles such as WC pans and washbasin pedestals. Then tape your felt-tip pen to a small offcut of wood and run the block against the skirting board and round each obstacle so that the pen can draw out their profiles on the paper (A).

A

2 Lift the template and place it on the sheet vinyl in another (and larger) room. Place a board offcut under the cutting line to avoid damaging floor surfaces. Use the same block plus a china marker (which won't permanently mark the vinyl) to scribe the room outline and the obstacle shapes on to the vinyl (B). As you move the block along, keep its edge aligned with the outside of the perimeter lines on the template, and with the inside of the lines around obstacles. Lift the template, and using your trimming knife and ruler, cut along all the lines. Make a release cut from the edge of the sheet into each enclosed cut-out.

3 Carefully carry the sheet vinyl into the room where it will be laid and fit it. You'll find that the release cuts let the sheet fit neatly round the obstacles (C), and the end result should be a perfect fit all round. Finish off laying the sheet vinyl by lifting the edges, applying double-sided flooring tape, peeling off the release paper and pressing the edges of the vinyl back into position.

B

top tip

Bathrooms, by definition, are wet areas, and if you have children in the family, they'll be wet areas with a vengeance. To stop water from seeping beneath the vinyl and possibly causing wet rot in the floorboards beneath, run a bead of clear silicone mastic all round the edge of the sheet to seal it to the skirting boards. Run it round WC pans and basin pedestals too. If there are any slight gaps due to inaccurate scribing or cutting of the vinyl, apply a bead of white mastic to conceal them.

C

woodworking 1

Even if you never do more than cut a shelf to length, you need enough woodworking know-how to be able to make a decent job of it. Some simple tips and a few basic tools will make it easy to get things exactly the right size, cut cleanly and squarely – just like the professionals.

MEASURING, MARKING AND CUTTING

Whether you're making something from natural timber or a man-made board, your first step is to decide how big each part is going to be, and to mark the dimensions on the wood. Get this wrong, and you're in trouble from the start.

Two things are really important. The first is to check that the wood you're working on is square – in other words, its sides and ends must all be at 90 degrees to each other before you start taking measurements from them. Do this by holding your try square against one edge of the wood with its blade in line with the adjacent edge. If the corner is out of square, draw a line across the wood against the edge of the blade with a sharp pencil or a trimming knife. Cut off the end or edge along this line (see steps 1 and 2 below).

The second thing to remember is that these adjustments actually cut some wood away. Start a saw cut, then stop sawing and measure the width of the cut you've made. It could be as much as 2 or 3 mm (⅛ in) wide, depending on the size of the saw teeth. This means that you must always saw on the waste side of your marked line so that the line forms one edge of the cut. Do this and every piece you cut will be precisely the size you want – not a millimetre more, not a millimetre less.

1 To cut a piece of wood to length, hook your tape measure over the end and pull it out to the length you want. Make a mark on the wood, then hold your try square against the edge and line the blade up with the mark so that you can extend the cutting line right across the wood. If cutting a sheet of

you will need

- **Length of wood**
- **Tape measure**
- **Sharp pencil or trimming knife**
- **Try square**
- **Straight timber batten**
- **Bench hook**
- **Portable workbench**
- **Tenon saw** *or*
- **Jigsaw**
- **Clamps**

top tip

Let the jigsaw do the work. If you force it, the blade will bend sideways and you won't get a square-edged cut. Jigsaws cut on the upstroke, so if your board has a 'good' surface, such as a veneer or laminate finish, place this face down on the bench. Any splintering that occurs will then be on the opposite face of the board and won't matter.

board, make two marks close to opposite edges of the sheet, then join them up across the board using your straight timber batten as a ruler.

2 **If sawing by hand**, a simple jig called a bench hook is the best way to hold the wood securely. It's a piece of board with two blocks of wood screwed to it, and you can make one yourself from scrap wood in a few minutes. Put it on your workbench with the bottom block pressed against its edge. Then hold the wood you're cutting against the other block, position your saw blade on the waste side of the cutting line and start the cut. Draw the saw back towards you gently three or four times, then start sawing for real with the saw blade at an angle to the wood surface (A). Level off the blade to finish the cut, letting it saw just into the base of the bench hook for a splinter-free finish.

If using a jigsaw, clamp the wood in the jaws of your workbench and line up the saw blade just on the waste side of the cutting line. Start the saw, then run it into the wood and cut straight across to the other side (B). Support the offcut with your free hand as you complete the cut so that it doesn't splinter.

You can also make angled cuts with your jigsaw. Adjust the baseplate to the angle you want – here it's 45 degrees – using the guide on the saw body, and saw away (C).

To make a long cut across a board, clamp a batten across it to guide the edge of the saw's baseplate and stop the cut from wandering off-line. Align the saw blade with the cutting line, slide the batten against one edge of the baseplate and clamp it to the board. Do the same at the opposite end of the cutting line. Then start the saw and run it against the edge of the batten right across the board (D).

go metric

When woodworking, you should really use only metric measurements . They're always whole numbers, which makes them easier to read off a tape measure, and easier to add and subtract than fractions of an inch. Although this book gives you imperial equivalents whenever metric sizes are quoted, the conversion can't always be 100 per cent accurate. Stick with millimetres and you'll find life far simpler all round.

B

C

D

woodworking 2

Lots of DIY jobs involve making holes in things. For example, you'll need holes in pieces of wood to insert screws, so that you can join them to other pieces of wood or fix them to the walls. You'll also need to make holes in the walls for the plastic plugs that hold the screws. In each case, you need the right type of drill bit to make the hole, and a power drill to drive it.

DRILLING HOLES IN WOOD

Use twist drill bits to make holes up to about 10 mm (⅜ in) in diameter. They come in sets, and you pick the drill bit to match the diameter of the screw you're driving. For larger holes up to about 38 mm (1½ in) in diameter, go for flat wood bits, also called spade bits because of their shape. These can be bought singly or in sets, but as they're quite expensive, it's best to buy them individually as required. Incidentally, you can use twist drill bits to make holes in metal and plastic, as well as in wood.

A

USING A TWIST DRILL BIT

1 Clamp the wood in the jaws of your workbench so that the drill can go through into fresh air (A).
2 Fit the twist drill bit into the chuck (the moving jaws) of your drill, making sure it's securely held and fitted straight. (See pages 54–5 for advice on choosing the appropriate drill bit for particular screws.) Select the higher speed setting if you have a two-speed drill. Position the drill so that the bit is resting on the mark where you want the hole, and start drilling.

USING A FLAT WOOD BIT

1 Secure the shank of a flat wood bit in the drill chuck as when using a twist drill bit.
2 Position the point of the bit at your drilling mark, check that you're holding the drill at right angles to the wood, and start drilling. Stop as soon as the point emerges through the underside of the wood.
3 Turn the wood over and drill back into the pierced hole on that side. This stops the wood from splintering as the shoulders of the bit emerge. Alternatively, you can get a clean exit hole simply by drilling straight through into some scrap wood positioned underneath the piece you're drilling.

DRILLING HOLES IN WALLS

You can also use twist drill bits to make small holes in plasterboard walls and ceilings, but for solid walls and the concrete lintels above windows you must use a masonry drill bit which has a specially hardened cutting edge. These, too, are sold singly, so it's best to buy just the sizes you use regularly, and to replace them when they get blunt.

USING A MASONRY DRILL BIT

1 Fit a masonry drill bit into the drill chuck and check that the chuck is tight.

2 Use a bradawl to make a drilling mark in the plaster. If fixing a timber batten to the wall, poke the bradawl through the screw holes in the batten to mark their positions on the wall (B). Work out how deep you need to drill (see pages 108–109), and wrap some tape around the drill bit this distance from the tip to act as a depth guide. Select low speed, if you have a two-speed drill, and position the drill bit at the mark.

3 Start drilling – slowly if your drill has a variable speed (C). Drill until the tape touches the plaster surface, blow the dust out of the hole and pop in your wall plug ready to receive its screw (D). If the wall crumbles away leaving a hole too big to grip the plug, fill the hole with filler, then start again.

4 Start the screw a little way into the wallplug and then drive the screw fully home into it (E).

B

top tip

Always secure wood to your workbench - either in its jaws or with clamps - before starting to drill holes in it. Otherwise the drill can snatch the wood from your hand as you start drilling, and cause you a nasty injury.

C

D

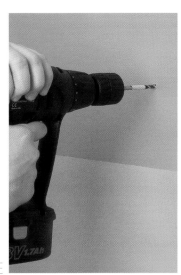

E

woodworking 3

Most of the wood you use around the house will be bought 'off the shelf' – already sawn and planed to a standard cross-sectional size. You just cut off the lengths you want. But sometimes that won't do because you need a piece of wood in a non-standard size, or you want to cut it into a shape instead of working with straight edges.

you will need

- Plane plus oilstone, honing guide and oil
- Pencil
- Jigsaw plus assorted cutting blades
- Scrolling jigsaw for tight curves
- Fine glasspaper
  or
- Orbital sander plus fine abrasive sheets to fit

PLANING WOOD

To make fine adjustments to wood, you need a plane. This tool contains a sharp cutting blade which is held at an angle to the wood surface. As it is pushed along, it slices off thin slivers of wood, which emerge in long, curly shavings through the opening in the plane body just above the blade. You can adjust the blade position to vary the thickness of the shavings, but you'll get better results when you're planing wood down to size by taking off several thin shavings rather than a single thick one.

You'll need to take out the blade and sharpen it from time to time. To do this, you need an oilstone (a small block of abrasive mineral), a clever gadget called a honing guide, which holds the blade at the correct angle to the stone, and some light household machine oil for lubrication. The instructions with the honing guide will tell you how to use it.

A

bench plane

B

jigsaw

C

jigsaw

1 To plane wood down to size, adjust the position of the plane blade so that it cuts nice, thin shavings off the wood. (If you try to remove too much wood with each pass, the blade will dig in and the tool will jump, damaging your work.)

2 Mark guide lines on opposite sides of the wood to show how far down you want to plane.

3 Hold the plane on the edge of the wood with the blade just clear of the end, and push it along the edge in one smooth movement (A), letting it run straight off at the far end. Keep the plane level as you work, and carry on planing until you're down to the pencil lines.

CUTTING CURVES

The jigsaw is your ally if you want to cut curves in wood or man-made boards (B and C). An ordinary jigsaw will cut quite tight curves, but for really intricate shapes you will need a scrolling jigsaw. With this you can actually turn the cutting blade to the left or right as you saw, enabling you to cut really tight curves.

1 To cut curves in wood or man-made boards, mark out the shape you want on the surface.

2 Then start the saw and feed the blade into the wood at one end of the cutting line.

3 Drive it carefully along the line, letting the saw do the work as you negotiate the curves.

SANDING WOOD

When you've finished planing and shaping your work, the final stage is to sand it smooth, ready for whatever decorative or protective finish you plan to give it. You can do this by hand, using sandpaper (often called glasspaper because the abrasive surface is actually finely crushed glass rather than the sand it used to be in the old days). Alternatively, you can save on elbow grease and use a power sander. The orbital type with a rectangular baseplate is best for flat or convex surfaces (D). For concave ones, fit a drum or flap sander attachment in your power drill.

orbital sander

1 To sand planed or sawn surfaces smooth, simply fold some glasspaper into a flat pad or hold it round a cork sanding block and rub it backwards and forwards until the surface feels smooth to the touch.

2 Blow away the dust, leaving the surface ready for whatever finish you want to apply to the wood.

If you have a power sander, you can use it to finish off flat surfaces, such as this alcove shelf – but you'll still have to hand-sand mouldings and fiddly bits that the sander won't reach. Fit the finest abrasive sheet to the sander, switch it on and sand away. Always work along the grain, never across it, or you'll leave scratch marks.

woodworking 4

Sometimes you won't be making things from scratch. Instead you'll buy what's called flat-pack furniture, which could be anything from a bookshelf to a kitchen cabinet or a wardrobe. The manufacturer has done all the hard work for you, and all you have to do is to assemble it. Piece of cake? Not likely...

you will need

- Flat-pack furniture (we chose a kitchen cabinet)
- Hammer
- Screwdrivers
- Patience!

THE TROUBLE WITH INSTRUCTIONS

Flat-pack furniture has three ingredients – the various panels, shelves, doors and drawers that make up the item, a bag of hardware for putting everything together, and the instructions. The parts and hardware are usually fine – holes drilled in all the right places, and a bit of hardware to fit every one. The trouble is working out what goes where.

In order to sell the flat-packs to markets other than the UK, the assembly instructions seldom include any words. What you usually get instead is an assortment of spidery drawings, often with little visible detail, to help you tell one fixing from another. The only safe way round this is to have a dummy run, laying everything out on the floor and matching a piece of hardware to every joint, door, drawer and shelf. When you're sure you know where (and how) everything fits, you can start putting the unit together for real. And if you really can't make head or tail of the kit, or there seem to be parts missing, simply pack everything up and take it back to where you bought it.

A

B

C

1 Take care when opening packaging with a knife not to damage any of the contents. Lay out all the panels and identify which is which. Next check off the hardware, counting that you have the correct number of all the fittings and identifying what goes where. Once this is done, you can start putting things together. Here the panel fixings need tapping in with a hammer to seat them in one component before the mating panel is offered up and the joint assembled (A and B).

2 With the basic carcass of the unit assembled, it's time to add the back panel. This stiffens the whole structure and helps to keep it square. The hardboard panel is simply fixed to the back edges of the carcass with panel pins.

3 Don't forget the plinth, which provides vital support for the base of the cabinet (C). It's attached with simple L-shaped metal brackets, but plastic joint blocks are sometimes used instead.

4 Hang the door after attaching the hinge to the door panel and the mounting block to the cabinet side (D). One screw on the hinge arm fixes the hinge to the block, while the other screw allows you to adjust the way the door hangs – a vital step if you're assembling a run of cabinets. This one is now ready to join its mates and get its worktop on.

top tip

Tall units, such as bookcases and wardrobes can be a bit unstable if they stand against a skirting board where carpet grippers have been fitted. Use hardboard or thick cardboard underneath the front of their plinths to get them dead level. For extra stability, you can attach two small L-shaped brackets to the top shelf or panel of the unit so the bracket upstands fit flush against the wall surface behind the unit. Then drive a screw through each bracket into a drilled and plugged hole in the wall to make the unit secure.

D

putting up
a fixed shelf

After painting and decorating, the next job every budding do-it-yourselfer seems to move on to is putting up a shelf or two. How you tackle this depends on where you're fixing the shelf. There are two basic options – to use brackets if the shelf is on an open wall, or to set it on wall-mounted support battens if it's in an alcove. Here's how to tackle either...or both.

you will need

- Shelves, track and brackets
- Pencil
- Spirit level
- Bradawl
- Tape measure
- Power drill and masonry drill bit
- Wallplugs (masonry walls only)
- Screws and screwdriver

USING SHELF BRACKETS

There's a huge choice in shelf brackets – mainly in metal, but you can also find plenty of wood shelf brackets too, often pre-packed with a matching shelf. You can make shelves yourself from natural wood planks, or buy veneered or plastic-coated boards in a range of standard lengths and widths.

How many brackets you need to put up depends on how long your shelf is and how heavily it will be loaded, but as a general rule fit a bracket about every 600 mm (2 ft) to be on the safe side. You also need good fixings – screws long enough to go into wallplugs to a depth of at least 38 mm (1½ in) in solid masonry.

1 To put up a fixed shelf, decide where you want to install it and use your pencil and spirit level to draw a faint horizontal guideline on the wall level with the shelf's top surface. Next, use your tape measure to mark the positions of the brackets on the line.

2 Hold the first bracket at its mark, check that it's vertical with your spirit level and mark the fixing positions on the wall through the screw holes. Drill and plug the fixing holes, then screw the bracket into place.

3 Hold the second bracket in position and rest the shelf and spirit level on top to double-check that the shelf will be dead level. Mark the position of the fixings for the second bracket as before (A), lift off the shelf and spirit level, and fix the bracket after drilling and plugging the holes as before. Finish the job by spreading a little woodworking adhesive on top of each bracket, then set the shelf in place.

A

USING ALCOVE WALLS

Alcoves are a great place to put up shelves because they have side walls to support the shelf ends. All you have to do is fix a slim wooden support batten to each side wall and rest your shelf on top once you've cut it to length. The only tricky bit is getting the two ends exactly level, but it's not that difficult when you know how. And you don't have to stop at just one shelf; you can fill your alcove from top to bottom, with shelves for books, ornaments, the hi-fi and anything else that needs a home. You can even fit shelves of different depth to match whatever you intend to store on them.

1 Prepare the two support battens – each about 25 mm (1 in) shorter than the shelf depth, and with its front end angled. Drill two holes in each one for the screws. Then hold one against the wall at the shelf position, level it up and mark the positions of the screw holes on the wall with a bradawl. Drill and plug the holes and screw the batten into place.

2 Use your spirit level and pencil to mark a faint line on the back wall of the alcove, level with the top of the first batten. Position the second batten level with this line on the other wall and it'll be level with its mate. Fix it in place, then measure up and cut the shelf to length. If the alcove isn't square, use a tool called a sliding bevel to record the corner angle and transfer it to the shelf end.

3 To stop the shelf from sagging when heavily loaded with objects, cut 75 mm (3 in) wide strips of MDF. Carefully glue and screw them to the underside of the front edge of the shelf (B).

4 When you've fixed all the battens you need, and you've cut and stiffened the shelves, lift them into place to check the fit (C). There's no need to secure the shelves in place by screwing them down. Leaving them loose means that you can easily take them off for painting.

you will need

- **Shelf materials**
- **50 x 12 mm (2 x 1 in) planed softwood for shelf supports**
- **Jigsaw *or* handsaw**
- **Bradawl**
- **Power drill plus masonry drill bit**
- **25 mm (1 in) No. 6 woodscrews**
- **Wallplugs**
- **Spirit level**
- **Pencil**
- **Tape measure**
- **75 mm (3 in) wide strips of 6 mm (¼ in) MDF**
- **PVA wood adhesive**

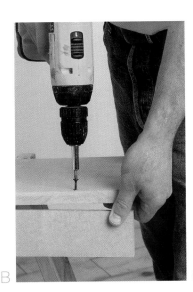

B

C

putting up
adjustable shelving

Fixed shelves are fine if you know what you want to put on them and you're confident that your storage needs won't change in the future. Many people, however, prefer their shelving to be flexible to their needs, and that's where adjustable shelf systems come into their own. The brackets simply slot into vertical tracks on the wall, allowing the shelves to be positioned – and repositioned – exactly as you wish.

you will need

- Shelf track and brackets
- Spirit level
- Pencil
- Bradawl
- Power drill and masonry drill bit
- Wallplugs (masonry walls only)
- 50 mm (2 in) No. 8 wood screws
- Screwdriver
- Shelves

TRACKS AND BRACKETS

There have been many variations on the adjustable shelving theme over the years, but the best is still the slotted steel track type with slim metal brackets to support the shelves. This system allows the shelves to be easily adjusted, and the positive locking action of the brackets in the slots ensures that they stay put. This system can be used on any type of wall, but if it is a timber-framed partition, you must locate the positions of the vertical frame members (called studs) and screw the tracks to these. Fixings straight into plasterboard will simply pull out as soon as you load up the shelves.

The tracks come in standard lengths, usually 1 and 2 m (about 3 ft 3 in and 6 ft 6 in) long. You can cut them down with a hacksaw if you need an exact but non-standard length of track. Brackets are also available in a choice of lengths to suit different shelf depths.

1 Decide where you want to fit the tracks, and how far apart to space them. Then use your spirit level and pencil to mark a faint horizontal guideline on the wall across the track positions. Hold up the first track length with its top on the line and mark the position of the

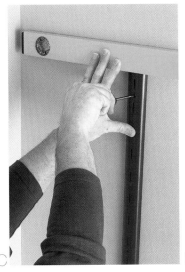

B   C   D

top screw hole on the wall with your bradawl. Drill and plug the hole, then drive the top screw almost fully home (A).

2 Hold your spirit level alongside the track and get it perfectly vertical. Then mark the positions of the other screw holes (B), swing the track aside and drill and plug them. Swing the track back to the vertical and drive in the rest of the screws. Don't forget to tighten the top one too.

3 Hold the second track level with the guideline at its chosen position (C), and repeat steps 1 and 2 to fit first the top screw, then the rest. Repeat the process if you need to install more tracks for a wide shelf arrangement.

4 Slot the brackets into the tracks at whatever spacing you've decided you need, taking care to use pairs of slots that are level with each other. Then set the shelves in place one by one (D).

top tip

Shelves that are out in the open – as opposed to within an alcove – could be knocked off their brackets in a collision unless they're heavily loaded. You can stop this happening by choosing a system with brackets that can be screwed to the shelves from underneath. Put the shelves in place, then press down on each one from above while you mark the bracket screw positions on the underside of the shelf with a bradawl. Screw the brackets to the shelves, using short screws that won't burst through the upper surface of the shelf.

putting up coving

If you've got cracks all around the edge of your ceiling, or you fancy finishing the room off with a decorative frame, then some coving is just what you need. It can be plain or fancy, and you can paint it in any colour you want to go with your décor. All you have to do is stick it up...

you will need

- Coving
- Pencil
- Timber straightedge
- Spirit level
- Adhesive
- Coving mitre box
- Fine-toothed saw
- Large filling knife
- Tape measure

A CHOICE OF TYPES

The commonest type of coving is made of plaster covered with thick paper, but it comes only with a plain curved surface. If you want something more ornate, look out for foamed plastic mouldings. The best are made from rigid polyurethane foam with a smooth surface, and are available in very good imitations of the traditional fibrous plaster mouldings found in many period homes. Avoid cheap polystyrene coving, which dents as you handle and position it and has a slightly textured surface. Both plasterboard and plastic types are stuck in place with special adhesive, but the plastic types are much easier to handle (and to stick) because they're very light in weight.

You buy coving in standard lengths – usually measuring 2 or 3 m (6 ft 6 in or 10 ft) – so you need to measure your room carefully, adding an extra 600 mm (2 ft) to each wall length to allow for cutting the corner mitres. Add up the total perimeter measurement and convert this into the number of lengths of coving you'll need for the job. Plasterboard coving is put up with a powder adhesive, which you mix with water to the consistency of porridge. Plastic coving has its own special adhesive, which you buy in tubs. Check on the packs how many metres each will stick, and buy enough for the job plus about 10 per cent extra.

1 With a helper, hold a length of the coving in the wall-ceiling angle and mark a pencil line on the wall along its top and bottom edges. Then use your pencil,

A

B

which mitre?

You need four different mitres to make corners – cuts 1 and 2 make up an internal corner, and cuts 3 and 4 an external one. Use these pictures to check that you're cutting the right one; you can waste a lot of coving by making mistakes. Note that in each of these pictures, the edge of the coving that will fit against the ceiling is positioned in the base of the mitre box.

straightedge (and spirit level for the wall line) to continue the lines right round the room. If the room is painted, score the surface with the corner of a filling knife between the lines to give the adhesive a good key. If the room is papered, you have to strip the area to which the coving will be stuck. Before removing any wallpaper, draw a line with a craft knife so you don't accidentally damage paper that will be below the coving. Then scrape off the wallpaper dry, without using any water or chemical stripper, again to avoid damage lower down the wall. Then mix up a batch of powder adhesive, if that's what you're using, or open a tub of ready-mixed adhesive otherwise, and you're ready to start putting the coving up.

2 Start fixing coving on the longest uninterrupted wall in the room. First, using a coving mitre box, make a type 1 cut for an internal mitre (see box above) on one end. Use your filling knife to butter adhesive along each edge of the coving. Press it into position between the pencil guidelines and hold it for a few seconds to allow the adhesive to get a grip. Scrape off excess adhesive and recycle it.

3 Make a type 2 cut on the appropriate end of another length of coving, and stick this on the adjacent wall to form the first internal corner (A).

4 Measure the distance from the square end of each length you've fixed to the next corner of the room. If either corner is less than two lengths away, fit a length with a mitred end at the far end of each wall. Then measure the gap between the two ends of the coving you've fixed, cut a piece to fit and stick it into place (B). If the corner is more than two lengths away, fit a whole square-ended length next, then repeat the above sequence – corner length first, then infill section – to complete the wall. Fill any gaps with adhesive.

top tip

If putting up plasterboard coving, tap masonry nails through the coving and into the plaster behind at 600 mm (2 ft) intervals to give each length some extra support while the adhesive sets. Pull the nails out when it has set.

putting up picture and dado rails

Picture and dado rails are right back in fashion these days, mainly because they break up big expanses of wall and give you the opportunity of using different decorative finishes above and below them. You can of course also hang pictures from a picture rail, instead of banging nails into the plaster.

you will need

- Pencil
- Spirit level
- Picture or dado rail
- Mitre box
- Tenon saw
- Instant-grip adhesive
- Tape measure
- Filling knife
- Wood filler
- Sandpaper

CHOOSING YOUR RAIL

A picture rail has a curved top, so you can hook S-shaped metal picture hooks over it and then hang your pictures from them. A dado rail is just a decorative moulding; its original purpose was to stop chair backs from damaging the plaster if they were pushed against the wall, and it's often called a chair rail for that reason. Both are available in several different period and modern styles; choose whichever suits your home's décor.

To work out how much moulding you need, simply measure up the room perimeter and add an extra 5 per cent to allow for cutting the corner joints. It's best to stick the rail to the wall with one of the new, instant-grip adhesives rather than using masonry nails, which can go in crookedly and force the rail off line.

Dado rails sit around waist height – typically 1 m (3 ft 3 in) above the skirting boards – while picture rails look best 450–600 mm (18–24 in) down from the ceiling.

A

1 Use your pencil, spirit level and a length of the moulding you're using to draw a horizontal pencil line right around the room at the appropriate level (A).

2 Cut a 45-degree mitre (see C on page 97) on one end of the first length of moulding, using a

mitre box and tenon saw. If it won't reach the next corner, simply apply a little instant-grip adhesive along the back and press it into place, aligning it carefully with the pencil guideline (B). Then butt-join the next length to the end of the first.

3 If the moulding is long enough to reach the next corner of the room in one go, measure the distance, mark it on the moulding and cut a second mitre facing the opposite way at this point. Then stick the length in place. Repeat the process on the next wall, butting the mouldings up against door or window frames. When you get back to your starting point the last length will finish with a mitred end to meet the mitre of the first length you fixed. Fill any open joints with a little wood filler, and sand it smooth when it's dried.

B

HEAVY PICTURES

If you want to hang heavy framed and glazed pictures or mirrors from your picture rail, reinforce the instant-grip adhesive with a screw driven in every 1 m (3 ft 3 in) or so. Pre-drill and countersink the holes in the rail, mark the fixing positions on the wall and drill and plug the holes. Drive the screws once you've stuck the rail in place.

top tip

When your mouldings are up, stick masking tape to the wall immediately above and below each rail, ready for the paint or wood stain you've chosen to apply. You can then decorate them really quickly, without any risk of getting paint or stain on the walls. And you get lovely, neat straight lines too!

putting up curtains

Like putting up shelves, hanging curtains is a popular follow-up to doing the painting and decorating – a natty bit of window dressing certainly finishes off a freshly decorated room, and new curtains deserve new track to set them off. The only problem you might have is making the wall fixings.

you will need

- Curtain track or pole set
- Pencil
- Spirit level
- Straightedge
- Tape measure
- Bradawl
- Wood screws
- Screwdriver
- Power drill plus masonry drill bit
- Wallplugs *or* spring toggles
- Hammer

TRACKS AND POLES

Modern curtain tracks come as kits containing everything you need to put them up. You can choose plain or corded sets, and you simply have to pick a length that can either be cut down or adjusted telescopically to suit the width of your window. Remember that the track or pole should project beyond the sides of the window opening by at least 150 mm (6 in) at each end to allow the curtains to hang almost clear of it when they're open.

Whether you pick a track or a pole to hang your curtains on, the support brackets must be screwed to the wall, although poles need fewer of them. What you need to know is what's spanning the window opening. It's likely to be a timber beam in older houses, and a concrete or steel one in more modern homes. You can drive screws straight into wood, but the other types of beam can be trickier to deal with. The best way of finding out what you have is to make a test drilling. If you hit solid material that's really hard to drill, you have concrete. If the drill goes through the plaster and into a void, you have a steel lintel with expanded metal mesh beneath the plaster. If you get soft grey dust and relatively little resistance to the drill, you have a steel lintel with a blockwork infill. Each needs a different fixing solution.

1 Start by unpacking your track or pole set and read the instructions carefully so that you can identify all the parts and work out how they fit together. If necessary, adjust the track length, and alter the cording from one end to the other. Then decide at what level to fix your track, and use pencil, spirit level and straightedge to mark a faint pencil guideline on the wall. Mark the positions of the brackets at the recommended spacings along the line.

2 **If your window is spanned by a timber beam,** make pilot holes with a bradawl, then screw each track bracket into place. Use screws long enough to penetrate the plaster – often up to 18 mm (¾ in) thick in old houses – and penetrate the beam by about 40 mm (1½ in).

A

If you have a concrete lintel, drill a hole at each bracket position, insert a wallplug and screw the bracket into place. You might find that the drill simply won't make any headway because it's hit a piece of aggregate inside the concrete. If this happens, try drilling a fresh hole close by – the exact spacing of the brackets isn't that important, and the drill will probably go in more easily.

If you have blockwork above the opening, drill holes as for concrete and insert wallplugs and screws to make the fixings.

If you hit metal mesh, drill a larger hole so that you can insert a spring toggle at each fixing point. Remove the screw from the toggle, thread it through the bracket and re-attach it to the toggle. Close the wings, push them through the hole until they can flip open, then pull them back against the inner face of the mesh and tighten the screw.

lifesaver

When you simply can't make any holes in a concrete lintel, try one of these alternative solutions.

If the curtain length hasn't been decided, position your fixings at least 230 mm (9 in) above the window opening so that they're above the lintel, and order curtains long enough to reach to sill or floor level as appropriate.

If the curtain length has been decided, try fixing a timber batten to the wall above the window using masonry nails rather than screws, then fix the brackets to that.

If all else fails, consider using a ceiling-mounted track which can be screwed to the joists through the ceiling.

3 When all the brackets are up, attach the track or pole to them. Poles usually just drop into their brackets (A), and may be secured there by a locking screw driven through the front of the brackets. Tracks clip into their wall brackets (B) and are held there by small rotating clips – you just rotate the lever from vertical to horizontal (C) to lock the track to them. Check that the track overlaps are the same at either side of the window opening and hang the curtains.

B

C

sanding a floor

If you want the good looks and easy-clean performance of a wood floor, it's well worth sanding the floorboards and then varnishing the newly sanded surface with clear (or even coloured) varnish (see pages 78–9). Although quite hard work, it's well worth the effort.

you will need

- Masking tape
- Hammer and nail punch
- Floor and edge sanders (hired)
- Coarse, medium and fine sanding sheets and discs
- Disposable dust-masks
- Safety specs
- Bin liners for the dust
- Vacuum cleaner
- White spirit and cloths
- Floor sealer
- Paint brush or roller

HIRING THE EQUIPMENT

As sanding a floor is the sort of job you'll probably tackle only once in a blue moon, it makes sense to borrow all the equipment you need from your local tool hire shop. Apart from getting an industrial-strength sander, you'll also get a smaller disc or belt sander to tackle the edges and awkward corners the big sander won't reach. Both machines come with a supply of sanding sheets and discs or belts on a sale-or-return basis, so you won't risk running out halfway through the job and you can take back any you don't use. The hire shop will even sell you a pack of disposable dust-masks and a pair of safety specs – both absolute musts, since this is one of the dustiest DIY jobs in the whole world.

The room must be totally stripped before work starts. When this is done, bring in everything you need for the job, close the door and stick masking tape all round it to stop dust spreading in to the rest of the house. Open the windows, switch on the sander and off you go...

A

B

1 Once you've stripped the room and lifted any existing floorcovering, inspect the floorboards thoroughly. Assuming that they aren't too gappy and are all securely fixed down, the main priority is to remove any old tacks or staples, and to punch in the heads of all the fixing nails to a depth of about 3 mm (⅛ in) or so (A). If you don't do this, they'll rip your sanding sheets to shreds as you work – especially annoying if it happens just after you've fitted a new sheet.

2 Attach a sheet of coarse abrasive paper securely to the drum of the floor sander. Tilt the machine towards you so that the drum is clear of the floor, start the motor and carefully lower the drum until it touches the wood. Be ready for the pull of the machine at this point – it can snatch quite fiercely as it makes contact. Move forwards slowly, working at an angle of 45 degrees to the boards so that you flatten off any raised edges (B). Then repeat the process by sanding along the line of the boards, first with coarse abrasive, then medium and finally fine abrasive. Don't forget to empty the dust bag from time to time.

C

3 Use the disc or belt sander to tackle the areas the big sander can't reach, again running through coarse, medium and fine abrasives in turn (C). Finish off by hand-sanding the room corners and the fiddly bits round radiator pipes and other obstructions. When you've finished sanding, vacuum-clean the floor.

4 Wipe over the floorboards with a cloth pad soaked in white spirit. Then apply the first coat of floor sealer, thinned with around 10 per cent white spirit to help it to penetrate the wood and give a good key for the second coat. Work back towards the door, and close it behind you while you wait for the sealer to dry.

the home doctor

Doing decorating and DIY for pleasure is not everyone's cup of tea. When something in the home needs improving, many people prefer to call in a little man (or woman) to tackle it for them. Fair enough – it's a free country. But sometimes things around the house go wrong suddenly, and you've no time to wait for someone to come in and fix it: you have to do it yourself. That's where this chapter comes in: it helps you to diagnose the problem and provides a prescription. It's a doctor for your house.

PROBLEMS AND SOLUTIONS

The Home Doctor features the most common problem areas around the house, so all you have to do is scan the checklist below and then turn to the relevant pages for help. There you'll find a range of symptoms described in a question-and-answer format, plus a brief summary of what's needed to put things right in each case. It also tells you how to cope with real emergencies, and what you should keep in your DIY first-aid kit so that you're prepared to act fast when you have to. It will help you to keep your house fit and well, whatever happens to it.

blockages

Where the water goes is a mystery to many householders. So long as it runs away every time they have a bath or flush the loo, that's okay. But if it doesn't, it's a problem. If a waste pipe blocks up, you're left with an appliance full of water. And if a drain gets blocked, you've got a nasty, smelly overflow outside the house to deal with. It's time for action.

Q: Whenever I take a shower, I seem to end up standing in an ever-deepening puddle that takes ages to drain away. What is going wrong?

A: You've probably got a waste pipe full of hair and scum (no offence meant). The trouble with shower trays is that some installers fit the trap, then the tray, and don't make any provision for reaching the trap later without dismantling everything.

• Make a wire hook small enough to pass through the plughole grating, and use it to fish into the trap for hair. If you catch some, pull it out and then fish for more.

• Look for an access cap (called a rodding eye) on the shower waste pipe outside the tray. If there is one, unscrew it when the shower tray has emptied and use some stiff wire with a hooked end to break up and pull out the blockage.

• If there's access to the trap beneath the tray, unscrew the trap and lift it out for cleaning.

• Buy and use a drop-in hair trap for the shower waste outlet. Remove any hair caught in it after every shower.

Q: I did the washing, and now frothy water is pouring out of the manhole at the front of the house and down the drive. What shall I do?

A: You've got a blocked drain. Thank goodness you didn't flush the loo!

• Don't empty any more water-using appliances.

• Locate the next manhole (if there is one) between the overflowing one and the road, and lift its cover. If it's empty the blockage is between the two manholes. If it's full, the blockage is further down the drain run, so look for the next manhole.

• Fetch your garden hose, poke the end up the drain from the empty manhole as far as you can, then turn the water on full to see if you can shift the blockage using water pressure.

• If this doesn't work, try the same trick by pushing the hose down the outlet from the full manhole. Feed the hose into its outlet before you turn the water on, or you'll blast the contents of the manhole all over you.

be prepared
Buy a set of drain rods for when the problem crops up again.

- Alternatively hire a set of drain rods from your local hire shop and screw them together so that you can poke the blockage out.
- As a last resort, call a firm of drain clearers.

A: The trap or the waste pipe is blocked, either with soap residues (bathroom) or solidified cooking oil (kitchen).
- Try using a sink plunger to clear it (A).
- If this doesn't work, put the plug back in.
- Place a bucket, a basin or some absorbent cloths (old towels are ideal) underneath the trap to catch the trap contents (see page 27), and unscrew its connections to the sink outlet and the waste pipe. Grip the knurled plastic connectors with a damp cloth if your bare hands can't get a good grip on them (B).
- Lift the trap clear, put it in the bucket and wash out any material blocking it up.
- If the trap's clear, poke some stiff wire – an unravelled wire coat hanger, for example – down the waste pipe as far as you can to try to clear the blockage.
- Reconnect the trap and pull the plug out to see if the water now runs away.
- Pour some boiling water containing washing soda down the plughole to wash away any remains of soap or fat in the pipework. Then run hot water through the pipe for a minute or so to make sure it's really clean.

Q: My bath/basin/sink won't empty when I pull out the plug. What's blocking it?

A

B

top tip
Don't try to clear blockages with chemicals that claim to clear blocked drains. They don't always work, and if that happens you end up with a sink full of strong chemicals to deal with as well.

SEE ALSO:
Leeks and Overflows – pages 140–1
Waste Pipes and Drainpipes – pages 26–7

ceilings

Ceilings are generally fine if they're left to their own devices. Their worst enemies are plumbing leaks in the floor space above, clumsy feet slipping off the joists in an unboarded loft, and old age if the house has lath-and-plaster ceilings and the plaster loses its key to the laths that support it.

Q: I've put my foot through the ceiling while clambering about in the loft. The hole's about 300 mm (12 in) long, with a piece of plasterboard dangling into the bedroom below. How can I repair it?

A: This, along with collapsing shelves, is a classic DIY sitcom disaster. This sort of accident is easily done and not too difficult to repair. Remember in future to walk along the joists.

• Buy a small sheet of plasterboard - you should be able to find a 1220 x 900 or 600 mm (4 x 3 or 2 ft) sheet in DIY superstores. Otherwise, scrounge an offcut from a nearby building site.

• In the loft, poke a bradawl through the ceiling at several points next to the joists that flank the hole.

• In the room below, draw pencil lines 25 mm (1 in) away from the lines of the bradawl holes, to show you where the centres of the joists are. Then draw two lines at right angles to these to frame the damaged area.

• Cut all the way through the plasterboard along the pencilled joist lines with a sharp knife.

• Use your trimming knife fitted with a small saw blade to cut from the hole out to each of the other lines, then saw along them and remove the rectangle of board containing the hole.

• Cut a matching-sized patch from your new board and nail it to the joists with galvanized plasterboard nails at each side.

• Tape all the joints with self-adhesive mesh repair tape, then apply a thin coat of ready-mixed plaster all over the repair with a plasterer's float.

Q: Cracks keep opening up all round my ceilings, and the filler I use always fall out. What's the answer?

A: The problem is caused by movement of the timber ceiling joists as temperatures and humidity levels change. This takes the plasterboard ceiling with it, and something has to give as a result.

• Rake out all the loose filler with the edge of your filling knife (A).

• Pipe a bead of non-setting decorator's mastic into the ceiling angle all round the room (B). Smooth it into a neat concave shape with a moist finger. You can paint over it if you need to as soon as it's developed a skin, which will take about 30 minutes.

A: You have two choices here. You can either copy the instructions above for patching a plasterboard ceiling, cutting out the old laths and a slightly longer area of the plaster, then letting in a new plasterboard patch. Or you can just slap on some fresh plaster and hope for the best.

• If possible, gain access to the ceiling from above and clear away the broken bits of plaster that once keyed the ceiling plaster to the laths.

• Brush diluted PVA building adhesive on to the exposed laths and the edges of the existing plaster.

• Buy a tub of ready-mixed plaster and a plasterer's float.

• Load up your float and push several generous daubs of plaster up against the laths so some is forced between them to hold the patch in place. When you've filled the area, smooth it off with your float and leave it to dry for 72 hours before painting it.

A: It sounds as though you've had a leak in the past – perhaps from a trap that's emptied itself and hasn't refilled if the basin isn't used regularly. A leak from the supply pipework would leave a permanent damp patch. Plumbing stains are notoriously difficult to hide with just emulsion paint.

• Check that the trap connections are tight, and run some water into the basin so the trap refills. Then you won't get drain smells in the room.

• Buy a proprietary stain sealer – usually sold in an aerosol – which you shake well and then spray on to the stained area. (Brush-on sealers are also available.)

• Cover the stained area with a generous coat of sealer.

• Repaint the ceiling with emulsion paint when the sealer has dried.

Q: **A patch of plaster the size of a dinner plate has come adrift from our old ceiling, leaving the wooden laths exposed. How can I fix it?**

Q: **I've got a nasty stain on the ceiling that's been there since we put a basin in the spare bedroom. It's not wet now, but it shows through every time I paint the ceiling. How can I cover it?**

A   B

top tip

For a cheaper alternative to proprietary stain sealer, use gloss paint as the sealer and apply emulsion.

SEE ALSO:
Floors and Ceilings – pages 14–15

condensation

When warm, moist air hits a cold surface, the airborne water vapour turns into tiny drops of liquid water. This film of moisture is called condensation. It's most obvious on windows, but it can occur on any cold surface around the house. The dampness it causes can encourage unsightly black mould to grow – not a pretty sight, and unhealthy into the bargain. But you can do a lot to discourage it.

Q: We have a fully tiled bathroom, and the walls run with water every time someone has a bath or shower. The kitchen's almost as bad whenever I'm boiling something. How can I prevent this?

A: Bathing and cooking are the two biggest causes of condensation in the home because they both generate huge amounts of water vapour. You need to get the warm, moist air out of the room as soon as you can, before it has a chance to condense.

• Keep the room door closed and the window open when you're cooking, and open the bathroom window as soon as you've finished bathing.

• Keep the bathroom warm all the time so that the tiles don't present such a cold surface.

• Get an extractor fan fitted to remove the moist air as it is created. You need one with an extraction rate of at least 30 litres (about 7 gallons) per second – check the fan packaging for details of its performance.

be prepared

If your home is a real condensation nightmare, consider buying an electric dehumidifier. It will dry the air and collect the moisture in its reservoir, and can be moved from room to room as the need arises.

A: It's condensation again, this time forming on a cold wall surface that's also poorly ventilated because the wardrobe is standing against it.

• Move the wardrobe to another wall in the room if possible.

• Otherwise, move it away from the wall slightly so that air can circulate behind it.

• Improve the ventilation in the room. The best solution is to fit so-called trickle ventilators at the top of the window frame. You drill a series of holes through the frame, then fit cover strips over them on the inside and outside. Leave the inner vent open so that there's a constant trickle of fresh air into the room.

Q: I've just moved a wardrobe away from an outside wall, and found patches of black mould on the wall behind it. Can I cure it?

A: Glass is a very poor insulator, so it gets really cold at night. Meanwhile, you're breathing out over ½ litre (1 pint) of water vapour every hour, and as soon as it hits the glass, it condenses. Stopping breathing isn't an option, but there are other solutions. Fitting some double glazing will make a huge difference.

• Go for so-called secondary glazing – new panes fitted to the window frame or within the window opening – if your windows are in reasonable condition.

• Otherwise have your windows replaced with new, maintenance-free double-glazed ones.

• Scrub the mould off with an old toothbrush, then wipe on a solution of household bleach diluted 1:5 with water and leave it to dry.

• Put masking tape on the glass to leave a gap of about 2 mm (just under ⅛ in) all round, then paint the woodwork to seal the rough surface of the putty in which the glass is bedded. This will discourage mould from forming there. You can also keep it at bay by wiping up any condensation with a dry cloth every morning – no water round the edge of the panes means no mould.

Q: My windows stream with condensation on winter mornings, and there's a line of black mould all round the edge of the panes. What can I do about it?

the home doctor

damp

Damp – water getting into your house where it shouldn't – makes life a misery. It creates unhealthy living conditions, and ruins decorations and floor coverings. It can also have serious long-term effects on the building, resulting in frost damage to masonry and rot attacking the woodwork. So if you have damp now's the time to find out why.

Q: I've found several damp patches on the back wall of my house, reaching to a height of about 1 m (3 ft) above skirting board level. Is this serious?

A: To stop your house from soaking up moisture from the ground beneath, it will (unless it's very old) have damp-proofing built into its structure. The walls will have a waterproof layer called a damp-proof course (DPC), and there'll also be a damp-proof membrane (DPM) in the floor if it's solid concrete. If either fails, or the DPC is bridged in any way, so-called rising damp will get in.

• Check the outside of your house to see if soil has been piled up against the back wall and, if it has, dig it away to at least 150 mm (6 in) below the level of the DPC – usually visible as a black line running between two courses of the brickwork.

• If you have paths or patios that are laid to a level that's close to the DPC, rainwater can splash off them and soak the wall above the DPC. Lower them if possible. Otherwise clear a strip measuring about 300 mm (12 in) wide next to the house wall and fill this with gravel so that the rain won't splash up.

• Inject a new chemical DPC into the affected walls, using pumping equipment available from tool hire shops (along with the waterproofing chemicals and full instructions).

A: You probably have rising damp in the floor, due to a failed or absent DPM, and having a non-porous floor covering has trapped the moisture underneath.

• Buy a damp sealer and apply it to the exposed concrete at the recommended coverage rate. This will form a new DPM and keep the damp at bay.

• Cover the new DPM with a thin layer of self-smoothing floor compound. This runs out in a thin film and then hardens to give you a new, smooth, flat floor surface ready for your new floor covering.

Q: I've just lifted some old vinyl flooring in the kitchen and the concrete floor beneath smells really musty. Have I got damp?

A: This is penetrating damp rather than rising damp, and is the result of defects in the building structure. You need to find the fault and put it right to make the house waterproof again.

• Use binoculars to search for any slipped or missing tiles or slates on the roof which could be letting rain in. Get a roofer in to replace them.

• Check that the strips of lead (called flashings) that waterproof the join between the roof and the chimney stack are correctly fitted. If they're loose, torn or missing altogether, water can trickle in at the join. Again, get a roofer in to fix them.

• Check whether gutters are sagging or blocked with debris – both can cause overflows and drench the house walls. Get your ladder out so you can repair any loose or broken support brackets, and scoop out dead leaves, moss and the like.

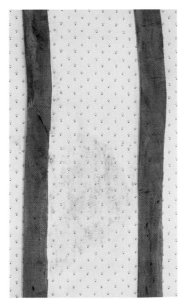

Q: Whenever it rains, I get several damp patches on the bedroom ceiling – one by the chimney breast, and another high up above the window. What should I do?

SEE ALSO:
Condensation – pages 126–7
Damp, Rot and Woodworm – pages 30–1
Leaks and Overflows – pages 140–1

doors

Nothing is more annoying than a door that's hard to open or shut. Doors can suffer from a variety of problems – some caused by everyday wear and tear, others by poor or over-keen decorating – but all are relatively simple to put right.

Q: I've got an internal door that catches the frame just at the top corner. How can I fix it?

A: This sounds like a hinge problem. Wear and tear or poor fixings can be the cause of the trouble.

• Open the door and check that the hinge screws are secure. Remove any loose screws and fit longer ones in their place.

• Check that the screw heads sit flush in their recesses. If they're proud or screwed in crookedly, the heads will clash as the door closes, stopping it from shutting properly. Replace any screws that don't fit in the countersinks in the hinges with screws of a smaller gauge number.

• If the hinges have been wrenched and the screws have torn out of the wood, use a couple of door wedges to support the door. Undo the hinge, drill out the screw holes and hammer glued dowel plugs into the holes (A). Chisel the plug ends off flush with the base of the hinge recess (B). Then drill fresh pilot holes for the screws and replace the hinge.

• If the hinges don't fit flush in their recesses, they'll bind and stop the door from closing properly. Undo them, chisel the recesses out a little deeper and replace them.

top tip

If you've got a warped door, the best solution is to replace it. The traditional remedies don't work quickly enough to be of any use.

A

B

C

D

E

A: Modern fitted kitchen units have hinges that you can adjust to move each door in or out and from side to side. All you need to be able to adjust them is a couple of screwdrivers: one for slot-head screws and one for cross-head screws.

• Open the door and you'll see that each hinge is in two parts. The hinge on the door is attached to the hinge mounting plate on the side of the cabinet by the larger screw you can see – the one nearer the back of the mounting plate. Loosen this (C) and you will then be able to move the door away from or towards the cabinet as necessary. Repeat the adjustment for the lower hinge as well.

• To move the door from side to side, again slacken off the larger screw (D). Then tighten or loosen the smaller screw and retighten the larger one when you've made the adjustment. Repeat for the lower hinge. You might have to make the adjustment several times to get the door hanging exactly in line with its neighbours (E).

Q: I've got several doors in my kitchen that won't shut properly and don't line up with the other doors. How can I get them to close properly?

A: Wood takes up moisture from damp air and expands slightly as it does so – often by enough to make a close-fitting door stick. It's a particularly common problem with back doors, which often open outwards and are even more exposed than front doors.

• Use a Surform planer file or a wood plane to shave some wood off the outer edge of the door so that it closes smoothly. Prime and paint (or varnish) the newly exposed wood at the earliest opportunity to make it moisture-proof.

• Take the door off its hinges so that you can paint or varnish the top and bottom edges – they're often left undecorated, and moisture can get into the bare wood there and make it swell, causing the door to bind. Clamp the door on edge in your portable workbench while you do this.

Q: My timber front and back doors both bind in their frames whenever there's damp weather about. What can I do to make them easy to open?

SEE ALSO:
Doors and Windows – pages 16–17
Draughts – pages 132–3

draughts

In a typical house, the gaps around doors and windows add up to a hole twice the size of your letter-box, and that's a big draught. Fitting draught-proofing all round will stop the icy blasts, and will knock between 5 and 10 per cent off your heating bill into the bargain.

Q: My front door faces the prevailing wind, and the hall is freezing when there's a gale outside. How can I keep my hall warm?

A: You have three areas to tackle here – the door head and sides, the door bottom, and the letter-box opening – and you need a different type of draught excluder for each.

• Buy rigid strip excluders with a flexible bristle or rubber tube seal for the door head and sides. Pin them to the door frame (A) so that the bristles or the seal is just compressed against the closed door.

• Buy an interlocking weatherbar and threshold strip excluder for the door bottom. Fit the threshold strip first, then attach the weatherbar to the door face so that the two components interlock to make a windproof and weather-proof seal.

• Buy a bristle-type excluder to fit on the inside of the letter-box opening, and screw it into place.

• If you have an outward-opening back door, either fit rigid strip excluders to the inside of the door frame so the door compresses the seal as it is closes, or fit self-adhesive rubber draught stripping in the rebates into which the door shuts.

safety warning

If you're draught-proofing a room containing a boiler or room heater, get your fuel supplier to check that there will be an adequate air supply for it to burn safely. This doesn't apply if the appliance has a so-called balanced flue and takes its air supply through that.

A

B

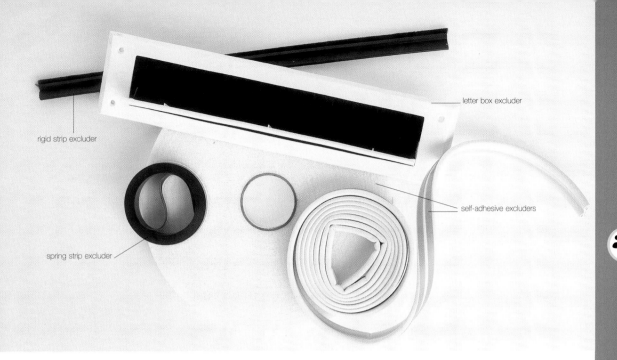

rigid strip excluder

spring strip excluder

letter box excluder

self-adhesive excluders

A: You need two types of draught excluder – self-adhesive rubber draught-stripping for the top and bottom, and the bristle type used for door sides (see illustration above) for the sides and centre rails. You have to fit some of the excluders on the outside.

• With the sashes open, stick a length of self-adhesive draught-stripping to the top edge of the upper sash and the bottom edge of the lower one so that they're compressed against the frame when the sashes are closed.

• Pin lengths of bristle seal mouldings to the inner sides of the lower sash and the outer sides of the upper one so that the bristles press against the window frame.

• Fit a length of bristle seal to the top edge of the lower sash and the bottom edge of the upper one so that the bristles meet when the sashes are closed.

Q: My old sash windows rattle to bits when it's windy, and they're really draughty too. What can I do to improve them?

A: The simplest solution is to fit self-adhesive draught-stripping all round. The latest synthetic rubber types are far more durable than the old, crumbly foam types.

• Measure the perimeter of an opening casement and a top vent (if you have them), and multiply the answers by the total number of casements and vents to work out how much draught-stripping to buy. It's sold in rolls, and the bigger the roll, the cheaper the unit price.

• Open each casement and wipe the paintwork clean. Then stick three lengths into the rebates along the top, the bottom and the opening edge so the inner face of the casement compresses them as it closes (B).

• Stick the fourth length into the hinge rebate so that the edge of the casement compresses it.

Q: I have traditional wooden windows everywhere, and not an inch of draught-proofing in sight. What should I use?

electrics

If you're confident enough to tackle electrics, there are several simple jobs you might have to do. And if you aren't confident, you still need to know what to do if all the lights go out. Follow my simple fault-finder and you'll soon have the power back on again.

Q: I've just cracked the plug on my power drill, and it's the factory-fitted type with no screws to undo. Can I fit a new plug myself?

A: Every new tool and appliance now comes with a factory-fitted plug. However, if it gets damaged, you'll have to replace it with a new plug which you'll have to wire up yourself.

• Buy a new three-pin plug with plastic sleeves fitted on the live and neutral pins (the shorter two), and check that it's fitted with the correct fuse – you need a 3-amp one (colour-coded red) for appliances rated at less than 700 watts, and a 13-amp one (colour-coded brown) otherwise.

• Unplug the appliance and cut through the flex close to the damaged plug.

• Hammer the old plug's pins to bend them so that if found by an inquisitive child, it can't be inserted into a socket outlet and risk giving a shock from the severed flex. Put the plug in the bin.

• Strip off about 50 mm (2 in) of the outer sheath from the appliance flex. Separate the three differently coloured wire cores inside and then remove about 12 mm (½ in) of the insulation around each one. Twist the fine wire strands together.

• Connect the cores to their correct terminals – BRown (live) to the Bottom Right terminal, BLue (neutral) to the Bottom Left terminal and green-and-yellow (earth) to the top terminal.

• Secure the flex sheath in the cord grip and fit the plug top.

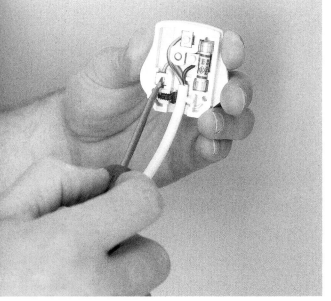

be prepared

If your system uses fuses, make sure you keep a supply of fuse wire or cartridge fuses to match the current rating of each fuseholder. Better still, have a spare fuseholder in each current rating ready to slot in when a fuse blows. **NEVER** use any other metallic object to repair a blown fuse. You could kill yourself – or someone else.

A: Replacing old light switches and socket outlets with new, fashionable versions is one of those uplifting finishing touches you can give to a newly redecorated room. It's not a difficult job.

• **Turn the power off at your main fuse box** (see pages 22–3).

• Undo the screws that fix the old faceplate to its mounting box, ease it away from the wall and loosen the screws holding the cable cores to their terminals. Discard the old faceplate.

• Reconnect the cores to the correct terminals in the new faceplate, copying the previous connections.

• Carefully fold the cable back into the mounting box and attach the new faceplate to it. Then restore the power supply.

Q: I've just finished some decorating, and the light switches in the room look really drab and old-fashioned. How do I replace these?

top tip

Use the old fixing screws if the new ones won't fit properly: this can happen when the new part has metric threads while the plugs in the old box have imperial ones.

A: Every circuit in the house is designed to carry only so much current without overheating. If you ask for too much by plugging in a lot of power-hungry appliances, the safety device in your fuse box or consumer unit will cut off the supply in order to protect it. This will be a wire or cartridge fuse in an old installation, and an electromechanical switch called a miniature circuit breaker (mcb for short) in a modern one.

• Unplug the offending appliances – things with heating elements are the usual suspects because they use the most power.

• Go to your fuse box/consumer unit. If you have circuit breakers, restore the power to the circuit by switching on the one that has turned itself off. If you have plug-in fuses, turn off the main switch first and then remove the fuse for the affected circuit.

• If the fuse is the rewirable type, loosen the terminal screws so that you can remove the ruptured fuse wire. Cut a piece of new fuse wire (you need the 30-amp rating for a power circuit) and fit it between the terminals.

• If the fuse is the cartridge type, fit a new fuse of the same current rating as the old one.

• Replace the repaired fuse in its holder and turn the main switch back on.

Q: I think I must have plugged in too many appliances at once because the power supply has cut itself off. How can I get the power back on?

SEE ALSO:
Electricity and Gas – pages 22–3

floors

Most homes have timber floors, covered with floorboards in older houses and with sheets of chipboard in newer ones. Ground floors may be solid concrete rather than timber, especially in houses built since about 1945. The commonest problems floors suffer from are creaks (timber) and surface deterioration (concrete).

Q: Our landing floor creaks loudly whenever anyone walks over it, however carefully they tread. How can I stop this noise?

A: The trouble with floorboards is that they can warp and twist, pulling up the nails that secure them to the joists beneath. When you tread on one, the board moves slightly and you get a creak. Chipboard floors can also creak badly if they weren't fixed to every joist they cross.

- Lift the floor carpet, if there is one. Then locate and mark the creaky boards.
- Hammer an old chisel or similar broad-bladed tool into the gap at the end of the board, and lever it up slightly (A).
- Protect the end of the next board with cardboard and prise the board up fully (B). Remove the old nails from the board (and from the joists if any have pulled through the board). Dust the tops of the joists.
- Replace the board and fix it to each joist with two screws at least twice as long as the board thickness. Use the old nail holes, unless they're badly splintered, in which case drill new clearance holes first (C).

A

B

C

A: Lumps and bumps will eventually show through sheet vinyl, as traffic moulds it to the contours of the sub-floor. What it needs is a new surface, and a product called self-smoothing compound is designed just for this.

• Mix the compound up according to the manufacturer's instructions.

• Pour it out on to the floor (D), covering a couple of square metres (say 20 sq ft) at a time.

• Trowel it out lightly (E) and leave it to find its own level and set hard.

D

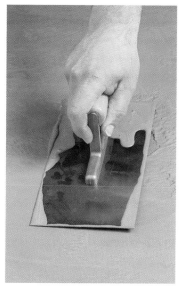

E

Q: I want to lay new sheet vinyl in the kitchen, but the old concrete is very uneven and lumpy and I'm afraid it'll show through. What can I do?

the home doctor

A: The trouble with concrete is that if it is trowelled too hard when it's first laid, cement is drawn to the surface and weakens it. Years of traffic then cause the surface layer to break up.

• Sweep or vacuum-clean the floor to remove as much dust as possible.

• Brush neat PVA building adhesive into any hollows to provide a good bond for the patching mortar.

• Fill any hollows with cement mortar, finishing the patch flush with the surrounding floor surface. Buy a small bag of dry ready-mixed mortar and add water to make up as much as you need.

• Dilute some PVA building adhesive with water in the proportions recommended on the tin for sealing concrete, and apply it to the floor using a paint roller – far quicker than using a brush. Alternatively, seal the surface with a proprietary concrete dust-proofing solution, again applied with a roller. Allow the sealer to dry for at least 72 hours before laying the new flooring.

Q: I'm having new carpet in the living room. When I lifted the old carpet and underlay, I found the concrete floor covered in grey cement dust, and several really crumbly patches. What should I do before the new carpet arrives?

SEE ALSO:
Floors and Ceilings – pages 14–15

leaks and overflows

Water, water everywhere, and all the boards did shrink (very Ancient Mariner). Plumbing leaks are always bad news: even small ones make a mess. Serious ones can make ceilings collapse and floorboards rot. They can happen because frost freezes a pipe, because corrosion makes a hole somewhere in the system...or simply because someone leaves the bath taps running unattended.

Q: There's a permanent pool of water on the path at the side of my house, apparently caused by a steady drip of water from a pipe sticking out at the eaves. What should I do?

A: The pipe is an overflow, connected to one of the water tanks in your loft. It's a sign that the tank is overflowing because of a malfunction in the valve that's supposed to fill it automatically and then shut itself off when the tank is full.

• Get up into the loft, taking a light on an extension lead if the loft isn't lit, and lift the lids off the big and little tanks: the former is your cold water tank, while the latter tops up the water in the heating system. You'll be able to see straight away which one is overflowing.

• If the float, which forms part of the valve, is partly submerged, it's probably punctured. Tie the float arm up to a piece of wood laid across the tank, then unscrew the float from the end of the float arm.

• Drill a hole in it so you can pour the water out, then screw it back on to the float arm and tie a small plastic bag round it to keep the water out. Buy and fit a new float as soon as you can.

• Run a cold tap for a while to lower the water level in the tank. Then bend the float arm down a little in the middle. This will stop the tank filling so full.

where to turn the water off

On a well-fitted plumbing system you should be able to turn off the water supply to various parts of the system in three different locations.

1 The main stoptap on the incoming supply pipe controls the supply to the kitchen cold tap and the pipes running into the tanks in the loft.

2 Gate valves shut off the pipes running out of the cold-water tank to the rest of the cold taps and to the hot-water cylinder.

3 Isolating valves fitted on the pipes that supply taps and WC cisterns enable them to be isolated without having to turn off the water elsewhere.

See pages 24–5 for more details.

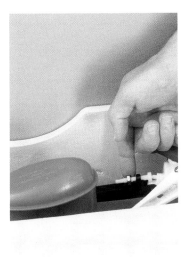

A: The problem is a faulty sealing washer on the inside of the cistern. Cost of washer? A few pence. Cost of plumber? Don't even think about it. You can do this yourself.

• Turn off the water supply to the cistern (see panel opposite). and flush the WC. Bale and mop out any water remaining in the cistern.

• Undo the nut that attaches the overflow pipe itself to the threaded bottom end of the overflow standpipe in the cistern.

• Next, undo the nut underneath the cistern that secures the standpipe to it.

• Lift the standpipe and its sealing washer out of the cistern. Take both to your plumber's merchant so that you can buy an identical new washer.

• Fit the washer, replace the standpipe in its hole in the cistern, tighten up its securing nut and reconnect the overflow pipe.

• Restore the water supply to refill the cistern, then check that the drip has stopped. Adjust the level of the float arm inside the cistern if necessary to make sure that the cistern fills to the 'full' mark on its rear wall (A).

Q: There's a damp patch underneath my WC cistern. It has a vertical overflow standpipe entering through the base, and water seems to be seeping out at that point. How can I make sure?

> ## be prepared
>
> Keep a pipe repair clamp in your toolkit. This will enable you to patch up a pipe leak even with the water supply still on, and could save a great deal of damage until you can get a proper repair made.

A: About 20 years ago, a batch of sub-standard copper pipe got on to the market, and ever since then, plumbers have been fixing the pinholes that this pipe is prone to develop. Let's hope this is the first and last one you'll suffer.

• Isolate the water supply to the affected pipe (see the panel opposite on Where to Turn the Water Off) and open the basin tap fed by the pipe.

• Put a wad of old towelling (or a bowl, if there's room for one) under the pipe where it's leaking, to collect the small amount of water still left in the pipe.

• Buy a pipe repair kit containing two-part patching putty.

• Clean up the pipe round the pinhole with fine abrasive paper or wire wool.

• Mix equal parts of the putty together and knead them well. Then dry the pipe and mould the putty around it, over the pinhole. Leave it to set hard (for as long as the instructions say) before restoring the water supply. The putty should last for years.

Q: I've been trying to find the cause of a leak in the bathroom that's leaving a spreading damp patch on the kitchen ceiling below. One of the underfloor pipes to the basin taps seems to have sprung a pinhole leak. How should I fix it?

the home doctor

SEE ALSO:
Waste Pipes and Drains – pages 26–7
Water Supply – pages 24–5

locks 1

When you're going out, you can lock and bolt all your doors and windows from the inside, apart from your front door which has to rely on external locks alone for security. Make sure yours are made to British Standard BS3621 and are stamped with the BS kitemark. If they aren't, replace them with new locks – something you should also do whenever you move house. You never know who's got a key to an old lock.

Q: I need a new mortise lock. Is replacing it a difficult job?

A: It all depends on whether you can find a lock that is the same size as the existing one, and with the keyhole in exactly the same position. If you can't, you'll have to do a bit of woodwork first to get the new lock to fit in the old slot (the mortise).

• Start by unscrewing the faceplate of the old lock (A). Then turn the key so that the bolt projects, grip it with a pair of pliers and pull the lock body out of its mortise. Choose a replacement lock that matches the old one as closely as possible (B). Make sure it has at least five levers inside – more secure than a lock with just two or three. The packaging will tell you how many levers the lock has.

• Try the new lock for fit in the existing mortise. If necessary, chisel out the sides, top and bottom of the mortise a little so that it slides in easily (C). You may also have to drill and cut a new keyhole in the door if the hole in the new

A   B   C

lock is in a slightly different place, and enlarge the shallow recess in the door edge that takes the lock faceplate.

• When you're happy with the fit, screw the new lock into place and test its operation by turning the key.

A: One of the simplest and least expensive security devices you can fit is called a sash window screw lock or dual screw lock. This is basically a steel bolt that passes through a hole in the inner sash and into a hole in the outer sash, preventing the closed sashes from being forced open. You fit them in pairs, one at each side of the centre bars (known as the meeting rails, because that's what they do when the window is closed).

• Close the window and drill a 10 mm (½ in) diameter hole through the inner meeting rail and on into the outer one to a depth of 19 mm (¾ in). Wrap a piece of masking tape round the drill bit, 29 mm (just over 1 in) from the tip, as a guide to help you drill to exactly the right depth. Drill a second hole at the other end of the meeting rail (A).

• Open the window and fit the metal keep plate over the hole in the outer rail. You may need to recess it into the wood if the sashes are a close fit. On some models of sash window screw lock, you push a small metal sleeve into the hole instead of fitting a keep plate over it.

• Reverse the sash positions and fit the threaded brass sleeve in the hole in the inner rail. Some sleeves need screwing in with a broad-bladed screwdriver (B); others are tapped in with a hammer.

• Close the window fully and insert a bolt, plain end first, into each sleeve in the inner rail. Then use the key provided to screw each bolt in until it enters the hole in the outer rail and its square head is flush with the sleeve in the inner sash. If the bolt won't screw in fully, remove it and shorten the plain end slightly by cutting through it with a hacksaw.

• Withdraw the bolts using the key to allow the window to be opened when necessary. Keep the key nearby so the windows can be opened quickly in an emergency such as a fire.

Q: I've got sliding sash windows that rely for security on just a flimsy catch on the centre bars. What's the best way of making them more secure?

top tip

If you're going away, screw the windows shut. Drill a hole at each end of the inner meeting rail and drive in a No. 10 or 12 wood screw long enough to penetrate the outer rail to half its thickness. Remove the screws and fit proper locks on your return.

A

B

SEE ALSO:
Doors – pages 130–1
Windows – pages 166–9

locks 2

Even if your front door has a mortise lock, it's a good idea to have a cylinder lock too. This keeps the door reasonably secure when you're in, allowing you to open it to admit callers without the need to use a key as you must with a mortise lock. It will also provide extra security back-up for the mortise lock – two locks are always better than one. As with mortise locks, fit a new or replacement cylinder lock that's made to British Standard BS3621 and stamped with the BS kitemark.

Q: What about fitting a replacement cylinder lock?

A: This is generally a simpler job. Make sure the new lock is a deadlocking type – either locking automatically when the door is closed, or else lockable with a key from either side. Some models can fit a door hung on the left or right; others are handed. Check before you buy.

- Firstly unscrew the body of the lock from the door edge and lift it off its mounting plate.
- Next undo the screws that pass through the mounting plate into the cylinder, remove the mounting plate and then push the cylinder from behind, out of its hole in the door (A).
- Fit the new mounting plate to

A

top tip

For extra front door security, fit a pair of hinge bolts to the hinge edge of the door. They're stout steel pegs that fit into holes in the door frame when the door is closed, making it impossible for a would-be intruder to kick the door off its hinges.

the door, using the longest screws possible to get a really secure fixing. Then compare the two locks so that you can see how long the flat connecting bar needs to be (B). Cut it to length with a junior hacksaw.

• Fit the cylinder into the door (C), offer up the lock body so that it fits on to the connecting bar and screw it to its mounting plate. Then fit the new lock-keeper to the door frame. Finally, don't forget to test the lock and ensure that the key turns easily.

B

C

A: There are locks on the market specifically designed for metal windows, but you might have to go to a security specialist rather than a DIY store to find them. One of the simplest – to fit and to operate – is a two-part lock. The fixed part has a projecting tongue that fits on the frame, and the swinging bar that fits on the opening casement engages over the tongue when the window is closed.

• Hold the part with the swinging bar against the casement and mark the

positions of the fixing screws. Make sure they're clear of the edge of the glass. Then drill the holes to the diameter specified in the instructions and insert two self-tapping screws.

• Position the part with the tongue against the frame and check that the swinging bar will fit over it. Then mark and drill the fixing holes as before and drive in the screws (D).

• Operate the lock by closing the window, swinging the bar over the tongue and driving in the locking screw with the key provided.

Q: What's the best way of making steel-framed windows more secure? All the window locks I can find seem to be solely for use on wooden windows.

outdoors 1

The outside of your house has to put up with everything the weather can throw at it, and every so often it will need a bit of attention here and there to keep it in good condition. Tackle problems when they first develop, rather than leaving them to turn into major headaches later.

Q: I've noticed water pouring over the edge of one of my gutters when there's heavy rain. What's the problem?

A: The gutter is probably blocked with debris – leaves blown by the wind, moss pecked off the roof by birds and so on. This stops rainwater from running freely to the downpipes, so it overflows upstream of the blockage instead.

• Set up your ladder so that it just reaches the eaves. Don't rest it against the gutter itself – you might crack it. Use a ladder-stay to hold the top of the ladder away from the wall if you have overhanging eaves.
• Scoop out the debris with a garden trowel or an empty can – just the right shape for a gutter scoop – and dump it into a bucket.
• Flush water from a watering can or garden hose into the gutter to wash away the bits you can't scoop out. Start at the highest end of the gutter run, and finish by checking that the outlets into the downpipes are clear of debris too.

Q: I have stained wood window frames which are beginning to look a bit dowdy. Can I smarten them up?

A: Unlike paint, which blisters and flakes off if it's neglected, wood stains weather by erosion – the coating literally wears away as time goes by. Fortunately, they're a snip to redecorate because, unlike old paintwork, there's next to no preparation required.
• Wash the surfaces down with sugar soap, rinse thoroughly them with clean water and leave them to dry. Then use fine abrasive to sand the surface lightly and remove any remaining sheen. This gives the new stain a good surface to stick to.
• Brush on a fresh coat of stain. That's all there is to it.

A: This mortar, called pointing, stops rainwater from soaking into the porous top surface of the bricks. If it's missing, the bricks can become saturated. In winter, the water they hold freezes and can split away the face of the bricks. Any missing bits therefore need filling as soon as possible.

• Remove any loose mortar from the affected joint using an old screwdriver and a paintbrush. Then buy a small bag of dry, ready-mixed mortar for pointing, a pointing trowel and a hawk to carry the mortar to the wall (you can use a board offcut instead if you have one handy).

• Mix up some ready-mixed mortar with water into a stiff paste in a bucket, and load some on to your hawk. Cut a sausage shape from the edge of the heap and press it firmly into the joint with your trowel. Smooth it off with the tip of the trowel to match the pointing in the rest of the wall.

Q: I've noticed a few places around the house where the mortar between the bricks has fallen out. Does it need to be replaced?

A: In older houses, the joint between a frame and the walls was often filled with mortar. This falls out as time goes by, leaving a gap that can let rainwater penetrate, causing rot in the frame and damp in the masonry.

• Rake out any loose mortar from the joint with an old screwdriver. Then buy a cartridge of exterior frame sealant (mastic) in a colour to match your woodwork – white for paintwork (which you can overpaint if you wish) or brown for stained frames. You'll need a cartridge gun to apply it.

• Cut the cartridge nozzle at an angle to give a bead of mastic a little wider than the crack. Then squeeze it into the gap, moving the gun along to extrude a toothpaste-like bead all round the frame. Smooth it off with a moistened finger.

Q: There are gaps round my door and window frames, where I'm sure water is getting in and causing damp patches indoors. How do I prevent it happening?

outdoors 2

Outdoor DIY doesn't just mean work on the exterior of a building. There are maintenance jobs to be tackled down the garden too – all part and parcel of keeping your whole property in tip-top condition.

Q: I have a boarded fence at the side of the house, and I've noticed that one or two of the boards have split and become loose. How do I repair them?

A: Fences spend their lives alternately getting rain-soaked and sun-baked, so it's little wonder that they eventually crack up. But fixing the odd loose board is no problem. Just buy yourself a bag of galvanized nails and find your trusty hammer.

• Prise out any nails that have worked loose in the wind. Then drive in fresh nails in line with the existing ones, which will tell you where the rails are on the other side of the fence.

• If the board is badly split or rotten, prise it out and buy a matching replacement from a fencing supplier. Cut it to length if necessary. Then tuck its thinner edge behind the thick edge of the adjacent board and nail it to the rails at top and bottom.

Q: My timber garden gate looks really tatty. What can I do ?

A: Garden woodwork weathers to grey as time goes by, and if it's in the shade, it can also become covered with unsightly patches of green algae. It needs a thorough wash, followed by a coat of wood preservative to restore its good looks.

• Scrub off algae with a diluted solution of liquid fungicide – the stuff used for cleaning paths and patios is ideal, or you can just use household bleach diluted 1:5 parts with water. Leave it on overnight to soak into the wood and kill the plant spores.

• Brush on a generous coat of wood preservative. You can get clear types, or coloured ones if you want to restore the wood's colour. Apply a second coat for maximum protection.

A: Most patios have been constructed so that slabs are laid on a sand bed. Lifting the old cracked slab and putting down a new one is a very simple job. What might be harder is finding a matching replacement. If this proves difficult, lift an existing sound slab from a less noticeable part of the patio and use this one to replace the cracked one. Lay the non-matching replacement where it won't be so obvious. Perhaps you could put a plant tub on it to conceal it even further.

the home doctor

Q: There is a cracked paving slab on my patio, caused by a plant container falling on to it from a nearby wall. Can I replace it?

• Prise up the old slab using a brick bolster and club hammer, taking care not to damage the edges of neighbouring slabs, and set it aside. Then rake over the sand bed and line up one edge of the new slab with its neighbouring one.

• Lower the slab into position and tamp it down all over with the handle of your club hammer. Be careful not to crack the new slab. If it sits below the surrounding slabs, prise it up again and add some more sand beneath.

A: Airbricks provide vital ventilation to the space underneath the ground floor. If they become blocked with debris, the underside of the floor structure can become damp. Then rot may begin to attack the wood with potentially disastrous results that can be very expensive to put right.

• Use a slim stick or garden cane to poke through all the holes of each airbrick and clear out any wind-blown debris. Check all your airbricks for blockages at regular intervals to prevent the problem from recurring.

Q: My house has a timber ground floor, and I've noticed a lot of cobwebs and debris blocking the airbricks around the outside of the house. Should I do anything about it?

radiators

If your central heating system was well designed and properly installed, all your radiators should be at roughly the same temperature when the system is running. If any are lukewarm or stone cold, it's time to investigate what's causing the problem. And if they've become a bit rusty over the years, now's the time to give them a fresh lick of paint too.

Q: My bathroom radiator is warm only at the bottom and doesn't dry the towels. How can I solve the problem?

A: There are several possible causes of cold radiators and towel rails. The best way of finding out what's wrong with yours is to check things out in a systematic way.

• The first thing to check is whether the radiator valves are turned on – you want maximum heat in the bathroom, so both should be fully open. You can open the handwheel valve by hand, but you'll need to pull off or unscrew the cap on the second valve on the other end of the radiator and then use pliers or a small adjustable spanner to turn its spindle fully anti-clockwise. Replace the cover when you've done this.

• Next, check if the radiator is full of water. When the heating is on, use a radiator key (if you don't have one, get a replacement from a DIY store) to open the air bleed vent at the top corner of the radiator (A). Have an old cloth handy as you do this. If you hear a hissing sound but no water emerges, there is either air in the system, or there's corrosion going on inside it, producing gases that get trapped in the highest radiators on the system. As the air or gas escapes, the radiator should begin to fill with water from the header tank. Close the vent as soon as water starts to trickle out. Catch the drips with your cloth.

• Go to your heating system's header tank – usually in the loft – and check the water level. It should be about a third full. If it's low or empty, push down the float arm on the ball valve and top up the tank. Keep an eye on it for a week or two in case the level falls again; this might indicate that there's a leak somewhere in the system pipework, which a plumber might have to locate and fix.

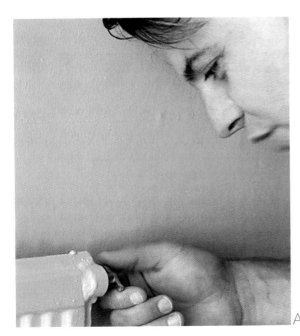

A

B   C   D

A: So long as old, cast-iron radiators are sound, there's no reason to replace them – they throw out a lot of heat, and they do have a certain period charm.

Q: I have old-fashioned column radiators, which I'm rather fond of, but they need a facelift. Can I repaint them?

• Turn the radiator off and wait until it's cooled down thoroughly – you should never try to speed up the paint-drying process by painting a hot radiator.

• Treat any rust you find with a proprietary rust remover (B), or else use a stiff wire brush to remove it.

• Treat any bare metal you've exposed by wire brushing with a coat of metal primer.

• Sand the radiator all over its surface to provide a good key for the paint.

• Use a radiator brush to paint between the columns (C). Don't be tempted to apply it too thickly, or you'll get unsightly runs.

• Use an ordinary brush to paint the other surfaces.

• The best way to paint the wall behind an old or modern radiator without splashing it is to use a slimline, long-handled paint roller as shown above (D).

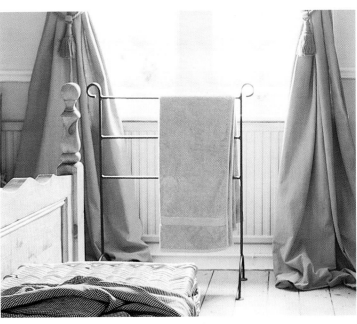

SEE ALSO:
Heating Systems – pages 28–9

rot

Rot attacks woodwork when two conditions are satisfied: the wood must be bare, and it must be damp. These conditions allow the plant spores that attack wood to land on the surface and start to thrive, reducing the wood to a soggy pulp surprisingly quickly. Act fast, or you might be too late.

Q: I've just noticed that rot has started to attack the foot of my garage door frame. How do I prevent it?

A: This is a classic place for rot to attack. If the garage floor is damp (garages seldom have a damp-proof membrane), rot can start chomping its way into any wood that's in contact with the floor.

• Scrape off the paint or stain so that you can see the extent of the problem. Then buy a rot repair kit, consisting of a liquid wood hardener and a two-part resin-based wood filler.

• Cut out any rotten wood. Then brush on the hardener and leave it to dry.

• Mix the filler and catalyst together (A), then use the spatula in the kit to apply the mixture to the damaged area (B). Leave it slightly proud of the surrounding wood.

• When the filler has set hard, use abrasive paper wrapped round a sanding block to smooth off the repair (C), ready for a fresh coat of paint or stain.

• If the frame is too badly damaged for filler to make it good, cut away the rotten section completely and replace it with new wood treated with preservative and screwed to the garage wall.

A   B   C

A: Wooden windows of all types are particularly susceptible to rot because they contain so many joints. Changes in temperature and humidity make the wood expand and contract. This breaks the paint film at the joints, allowing water to penetrate and rot to get started. Unless the paintwork is kept in perfect condition, the rot can then spread beneath the paint to other parts of the window.

• Insert the tip of a sharp knife into the wood to locate how far the rot has spread. Then strip the paint from the affected area and treat any damaged wood with hardener from a rot repair kit. Brush clear wood preservative on to the surrounding sound areas of wood.

• Prime and repaint the window, taking the paint film just on to the glass to seal the junction between glass and putty – masking tape on the glass will help you to do this neatly.

• Check the condition of your windows regularly so that you can touch up any breaks that occur in the paint film, and try to keep the rot from getting a toehold in the future.

Q: My traditional sash windows are showing signs of rot where the glazing bars intersect with each other and with the main frame members. How should I tackle this?

A: It sounds very much as though you've got an attack of dry rot – the nastiest of all the wood-destroying fungi around. It sucks moisture out of the wood, leaving it dry, brittle and cracked across the grain into characteristic cube shapes. It spreads by sending out shoots – the cobwebby bits you've got – that can cross masonry in search of fresh wood to attack. This calls for drastic action.

• Tear out all the affected wood, including the joists, and dispose of it carefully. Either put it all on a bonfire, if you're allowed to have one, or take it to your local authority waste disposal facility.

• Use a gas blowlamp or a hot air gun on its highest setting to burn off all traces of the cobwebs from the masonry above and beneath the floor. Take care not to set fire to any sound nearby wood.

• Brush liquid dry rot killer (available from builder's merchants) onto all the exposed masonry and any remaining sound timber in the area.

• Use only preservative-treated wood to replace components you had to remove earlier.

• Keep a close eye on the area to make sure the fungus doesn't show any signs of returning.

Q: I've just stripped out the boxed-in area underneath the stairs in an old house I've just bought, and have found rotten floorboards and horrible-looking strands of cobwebby stuff. What's the best solution?

the home doctor

SEE ALSO:
Staining/Varnishing Woodwork – pages 80–1

151

skirtings and architraves

Skirting boards and architraves aren't just there for decoration. Skirtings protect the bottom edge of the wall plaster from being damaged by furniture or feet, while architraves conceal the join between door frames and the surrounding wall. If they've been knocked about a bit or just look unfashionable, replacing them isn't difficult.

Q: I have plain skirting boards at the moment and I'd like something a bit more decorative. Is this going to be complicated?

A: There's a huge range of different skirting-board styles available, in primed MDF as well as in softwood, and in hardwood – the height of luxury – if you want the real wood look in your home. Make a note of the wall lengths so that you can buy pieces long enough to run from corner to corner without joins.

• Use a brick bolster and club hammer to prise off the old skirting boards. Slip a board offcut behind the lever to avoid damaging the plaster as you work your way round the room.

• Pull out any old fixing nails that remain embedded in the walls. If you can't shift them, hammer them from side to side until they snap.

• Cut a board to fit the first wall length and set it in place – don't fix it yet, though.

• Draw the profile of the skirting on the end of the next board and cut along the line with a coping saw.

• Cut the board to the length you need and butt it up against the first length so the scribed end fits neatly over it (A). Fix this board to the wall with screws or masonry nails.

• Repeat this process for the other walls until you return to the first board. If you encounter any external corners on the way, cut mitres to

A

make the corner joint, using a mitre saw jig (B) or a jigsaw set to cut at 45 degrees (see page 101). Glue the join when you fit the boards.

• When you get to the first board, remove it and scribe its end to fit over the last board you fitted on the adjacent wall. Then fix it as before to complete the job.

• Cover all the screw or nail heads with filler (or wood stopping if you're having a stained or varnished finish on the boards).

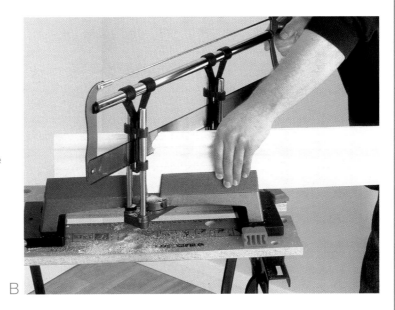

B

A: Choose replacements to match the room style, then measure the existing architraves so that you know how much moulding to buy.

• Prise off the existing architrave mouldings by inserting a wide chisel between wall and architrave.

• Hold a length of new moulding in place at one side of the door opening and mark the position of the inner end of the mitre cut on it. Cut the mitre, then repeat the process with another length of moulding on the other side of the opening. Nail the two lengths in place to the edge of the door frame.

• Hold a length of moulding upside down across the top of the two side pieces and mark its length directly from their top corners (C). Cut the mitres and fit the top section in place.

• Drive a panel pin down through each end of the top moulding and into the side of pieces to keep the joint closed. Fill any slight gaps at the mitre joints with flexible wood filler.

C

Q: Moving furniture around over the years has knocked bits out of several of our door architraves. How do I go about replacing them?

top tip

If you can't find the skirting board design you really want, you can create your own by adding period-style architrave mouldings along the top edge of plain skirting boards.

staircases 1

Your staircase is the most complex bit of carpentry in the house. Even a simple straight flight of stairs is made up of about 100 separate pieces of wood. It also carries a lot of foot traffic every day. So it's small wonder that it creaks and groans as it gets older. It needs a bit of first aid.

Q: My stairs creak so much that they're driving me mad. I'm having new stair carpet soon and want to fix them before the carpet goes down. Is it a big job?

A: This is the perfect chance to give your stairs the attention they need. What you can do depends on whether you can get at the underside of the flight from an understairs cupboard. If you can, start work there.

• You'll see that the ends of each tread and riser (the vertical bits between the treads) fit into slots in the main side supports (called the strings). They're held in place with slim wooden wedges, which might be loose or might even have fallen out. The horizontal wedges are longer than the vertical ones, which are driven in first and then held in place when the horizontal ones are fitted. Glue the wedges before tapping them back into place.

• Next, drill two clearance holes up through each tread about 9 mm (⅜ in) from its rear edge, and drive in 50 mm (2 in) screws to lock it to the riser above.

• Look for any blocks of wood that were once glued into the internal angles between the treads and risers, but which might have fallen to the floor beneath the stairs. These were also used to lock the stair components together and stop them moving and creaking as you use the stairs. They need to be reinstated so apply woodworking adhesive to their faces, put them back into their original positions and secure them

A there with a nail (A).

A: If the underside of the flight is boxed in, you'll have to do the fixing work from above the stairs.

• Squirt some PVA woodworking adhesive into the gap at the back of each tread so that it can flow down into the joint and bond the two components together (B).

• To reinforce the action of the adhesive, screw a pair of small steel repair brackets into each internal angle between tread and riser (C).

• To fix each tread to the riser below, drill a couple of clearance holes for the screw shank and countersink holes for its head down through the front of the tread. Then drive in 50 mm (2 in) screws to lock the two components together (D).

Q: I can't get access to the underside of the stairs to stop them squeaking. What's the best plan of action?

B

C

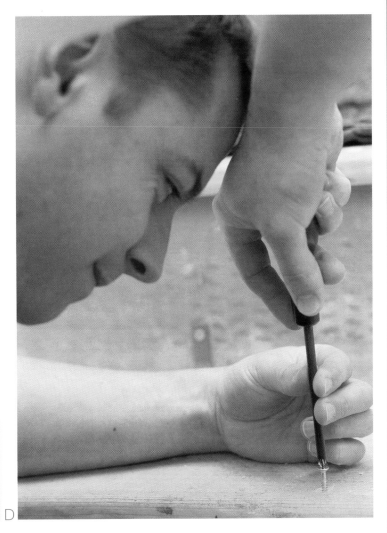
D

staircases 2

Sometimes a staircase might be sound enough, but the balustrade – the handrail and whatever fills the space between it and the stairs – might be well past it. Fitting a new one could give the whole stairwell a much-needed make-over.

Q: The handrail on my staircase is in poor condition after years of wear and overpainting, and the balustrade has been boarded over on both sides. Do I need to replace the whole thing?

A: You might find that you don't need to replace the whole staircase. Just removing the cladding can make a huge difference to the appearance of a staircase and increase the light enormously (cladding was often used to box in balusters and thus reduce painting time). If you're not happy with the effect, then go for a new balustrade. This would once have been a job for a skilled carpenter, but nowadays you can buy all the components you need for a staircase make-over from DIY superstores. You just have to work out how many of each component you need. You can measure up the handrail easily enough, and the length of the flight will determine how many balusters and spacers you need – balusters must be no more than 100 mm (4 in) apart to satisfy the requirements of the Building Regulations.

• Start by removing the cladding on the balustrade. Then saw through the centre of each of the balusters and wrench out the cut sections. Lever out the pinned-on timber fillets between the bases of the balusters.

• Cut through the handrails next to the newel posts – the main support posts at the top and bottom of the flight and at any changes of direction on landings. Use a hacksaw if you hit concealed metal fixings.

• Finally, saw squarely through the newel posts if you are replacing them. The makers of the replacement components you're using will specify exactly where you should make the cut.

• Fit the newel post extensions first, using the large-diameter wooden dowel in your kit to link it to the stump of the existing post. Make sure that each post is truly vertical by checking with a spirit level.

• You might find that you need to add a capping moulding to the top of the staircase string to receive the feet of the balusters, if the kit requires it.

• Cut each length of handrail to fit, using a tool called a sliding bevel to transfer the cutting angle from the old rail to the ends of the new one. Fix each length between the newel posts using the brackets supplied with the kit. Check that each section is parallel with the top of the string below.

• Start fitting the balusters, again using the sliding bevel to mark the cutting angle so that it matches the slope of the string and handrail. Slide each baluster into place after fitting a spacer fillet between it and its neighbour, and nail its top end to the underside of the handrail.

• With the construction complete, all that remains is to sand the surfaces with fine abrasive, wipe them with a rag soaked in white spirit to remove greasy finger marks, and to varnish or paint the new balustrade to suit your décor.

taps

Fixing problems with taps requires a bit of basic plumbing skill and a few simple tools. It's well worth trying to tackle them yourself because the spare parts you need are very cheap, while the plumber to fit them is very expensive. It's definitely a good time to DIY.

Q: I have several dripping taps around the house that waste a lot of water and leave nasty stains. Is there an easy solution?

A: Taps suffer a lot of hard wear, getting turned on and off many times each day. Sooner or later, they start to drip, and then everyone makes matters worse by screwing the tap handle down harder and harder in a misguided attempt to stop it. This just makes things worse. What's needed is some simple first aid.

• Check the type of the tap that's dripping. Taps that turn on and off with a quarter turn of the handle contain ceramic discs inside a special replaceable cartridge. Taps that take several turns have rubber sealing washers inside – usually 12 mm (½ in) across in single sink or basin taps, and 18 mm (¾ in) in bath taps. Mixer taps might have smaller washers, so buy a selection of sizes to cover every eventuality.

• Turn off the water supply to the tap. If you're lucky, there'll be a small isolating valve on the supply pipe; turn it off by rotating the small valve ball a quarter turn with a screwdriver. Otherwise you'll have to turn the supply off elsewhere – see pages 24–5 and 138 for details. Open the tap fully.

• Remove the screw handle – either by simply pulling it upwards or, if this

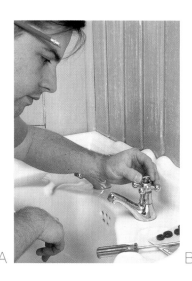

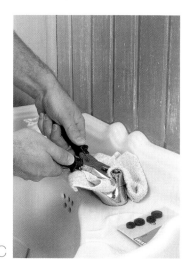

A   B   C

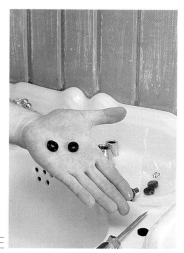

D   E

the home doctor

fails, by prising out the hot/cold indicator disc (A) and undoing the small screw underneath it (B).

• With an old-style tap, release the handle by undoing the small grub screw set in its underside.

• Then unscrew the bell-shaped cover. Protect the plating with a cloth if you have to use pliers or a spanner to shift it (C).

• Undo the tap headgear by gripping its hexagonal section and turning it anti-clockwise (D). Then lift it out of the tap body.

• Prise off the washer and fit a replacement of the same size (E).

The washer might be a push-fit, or might be held on by a small nut.

Re-assemble the tap, following the steps in reverse order and restore the water supply.

Q: Water seeps out around the bottom of the swivel spout on my kitchen mixer tap. Can I repair this?

A: This problem is caused by faulty O-ring seals on the end of the spout. You can replace them without having to turn off the water supply; just make sure both taps are turned off.

• Look for a small grub screw securing the spout to the tap body, and undo it so that you can lift the spout out of the tap body. If there isn't a grub screw, rotate the spout so that it's parallel with the tap body and pull it sharply upwards.

• When you've managed to pull the spout away, remove the faulty rings, buy spares of the same size and roll them into place. Smear some special plumber's silicone grease over the rings to make sure that they turn easily. Refit the spout to the tap and the job's done.

SEE ALSO:
Leeks and Overflows – pages 138–9

walls 1

You'll have come face to face with your walls during various home decorating projects, so you'll have already tackled the everyday defects, such as cracks and dents in the plaster, that walls acquire as time goes by (see pages 66–7). One type of wall finish that can require extra remedial work is ceramic tiling. You might need to replace one or two damaged tiles, cover an old tiled surface with some new tiles, or hack the whole lot off and replace them with something else.

Q: I have cracked one of the tiles in the splashback behind the bathroom sink while trying to drill a hole for the toothbrush holder. What are the chances of replacing it?

A: So long as you have a spare tile, replacing the damaged one is a simple job (A). And if you can't get a matching replacement, fit a contrasting one instead.

• Use a club hammer and a cold chisel – a specially designed steel tool for cutting into masonry – to chop off the old tile. If it's an edge tile, work inwards from the edge (B). Otherwise start in the centre of the damaged tile and work out towards its neighbours. Take care not to let the chisel slip and damage any of them as you work.

• When you've removed the bits of old tile, chisel as much of the old tile adhesive as possible off the wall surface to create room in the recess for the new adhesive.

• Use a screwdriver blade or similar tool to scrape the old grout off the edges of the tiles surrounding the recess.

• Spread some tile adhesive on the back of the replacement tile (C) and press it into position. (You can buy a small tube of adhesive for repair jobs like this.) Make sure the tile sits flush with its neighbours. Insert plastic tile spacers or matchsticks into the gaps to stop the new tile from slipping out of position.

• Allow 24 hours for the adhesive to set. Then remove the spacers and

A

B

fill the gaps all round the tile with grout (you can use the tube adhesive for this job too). Finish the joints neatly by drawing a fingertip along the lines (D).

• Next time you try drilling into tiles, stick some masking tape over the hole position to stop the masonry drill bit (I recommend using a new one) from skating on the glazed surface when you start the drill up. Drill very slowly until the tip of the bit breaks through the glaze, and you won't crack the tile.

C

D

A: No problem. You don't have to remove the existing tiles as modern tile adhesives are strong enough to allow you to stick new tiles on top of old ones. However, you'll have to disguise the double thickness of tiles along any visible edges of the tiled area by sticking on timber mouldings, ceramic tile edge trims or something similar. You can, of course, do this only the once.

• Wash the tiles down thoroughly with a solution of sugar soap or, if you don't have any, a strong household detergent will do to remove all traces of grease. Give the surfaces a good rinse with clean water and allow them to dry completely.

• Apply a strip of tile adhesive to the existing tiles all the way along the splashback using a notched spreader: make sure the strip is wide enough to take the first row of new tiles.

• Press the first row of tiles firmly into place above the worktop, using tile spacers to keep the gaps even all the way along. Check that the faces of all the tiles are flush with one another by holding a ruler or spirit level on edge against them.

• Stick on as many more rows of tiles as you need to cover the existing ones, cutting tiles where necessary to fit at the ends of the rows. Remember – a tile cutting jig (see page 91) is the best tool for this, especially if you are using thick or hand-made tiles.

• Finish off the top and side edges of the tiles by sticking on a timber or ceramic moulding with instant-grip adhesive.

Q: I have very old-fashioned black and white tiles above the worktops in my kitchen and I'd prefer something more cheerful. Can I cover them?

the home doctor

SEE ALSO:
Tiling Walls – pages 90-1

walls 2

If you have areas of tiling that you can't bear to live with, or the tiles have already been tiled over (you can do this only once), you have no choice but to hack the whole lot off. They might come off easily if they weren't stuck very well in the first place, but it's more than likely that the walls will be left in no fit state for either painting or paper-hanging.

Q: I hacked off the waist-high wall tiles that someone thought would look good in our hallway, and I've made a fair mess of the plaster. What can I do about It?

A: This usually happens when you strip off old tiles. Unless you're a natural at plastering, you'll either have to employ a professional to give the walls a fresh skim coat, or go for a cover-up.

• Put up a dado rail (see pages 114–15) to disguise the top of the wall lining.

• Buy enough sheets of plasterboard to cover the damaged area – you can get 1800 x 900 mm (6 x 3 ft) sheets, which will minimize cutting and wastage if you fit the dado rail exactly 900 mm (3 ft) above the top edge of the skirting board. You'll also need a cartridge gun and a couple of cartridges of instant-grip adhesive. Get the solvent-free type if you can – just as effective as the solvent-based versions, and a lot less smelly and unpleasant to use indoors.

• Assuming the wall is at least 1800 mm (6 ft) long, apply S-shaped swirls of adhesive to the back of the first board and press it into place. Cut other boards to length as necessary to complete the wall lining and stick them in place too.

• Fill the joints between the boards with decorator's mastic, and also run a bead of this along the edges where the sheets meet the skirting board and dado rail. Smooth the bead off neatly with a wetted finger.

• Give the boards a coat of emulsion paint when the mastic has developed a skin – usually within 30 minutes. Apply a second coat after about 4 hours.

Another way of covering up the wall and creating an upmarket effect is by using timber panels.

• Create the wall panelling effect by sticking on lengths of timber door panel beading. Buy these in self-adhesive kits for giving flush doors the panelled look.

• Mark the position of the first panel on the wall using a pencil, ruler and spirit level.

• Peel off the backing tape and stick each length of beading into position to make up the first panel. Measure the width of the finished panel and mark the positions for the other panels on the wall at regular intervals (A).

• Add further panels along the wall in line with the marks (B). Finish off by painting the wall and the beading (C). You can experiment with special paint effects inside the panels, or highlight the wood in a different colour.

A

B

C

A: Getting tiles off plasterboard is very difficult without irreparably damaging the board surface, especially if it wasn't sealed first.

• Try prising off one or two tiles to see how well they're stuck. You might be lucky and find that they come away fairly easily...but it's unlikely.

• If the tiles bring the surface of the board away with them, as they probably will, the quickest solution is to hack them away and then pull off the damaged plasterboard too. Pull out all the old fixing nails.

• Cut and fit a new piece of plasterboard in its place, and seal its surface with two coats of emulsion paint. Then fix your new tiles.

Q: I want to replace the tiles in a shower cubicle where one side wall of the shower is a timber-framed partition. Is this going to be difficult?

WCs

The only part of your WC that's likely to give you any trouble is the cistern. If you lift off the lid you'll see two separate mechanisms – the siphon unit that delivers water to the pan when you operate the flush lever, and the float-operated valve (often called the ball valve) that refills the cistern automatically after flushing.

Q: My WC seems to need more and more vigorous operation of the flush handle to get it to work. Do I need a plumber?

A: If you find that you have to press the handle several times in quick succession before the system will flush, it's likely that the piston flap valve is worn. This lifts water up inside the siphon unit and starts the siphonic action. A replacement costs only a few pence, so don't even think of calling in a plumber to fit it. You can do this, even if you have a close-coupled suite with the cistern mounted on the pan.

- Turn off the water supply to the cistern (see pages 24–5 and 138). Flush it, then lift off the lid and bale and mop out the rest of the water inside.
- Disconnect the water supply by undoing the pipe connector that screws on to the threaded end of the ball valve.
- Disconnect the overflow pipe in a similar way.
- Reach underneath the rear of the pan and locate the two wing nuts that secure the cistern to the pan. Undo them and set them aside.
- Undo the screws securing the cistern to the wall behind it. Now you can lift off the cistern.
- Turn the cistern upside-down and unscrew the large retaining nut that secures the siphon unit (A). Set it and the metal clamp plus its two bolts aside.
- Release the piston lifting arm from the flush lever rod (B). Disconnect the C-shaped wire linkage between the piston lifting arm and the top end of the piston in the siphon unit (C).
- Lift the complete siphon unit out of the cistern so that you can gain access to the piston and the plastic

A

B

flap valve that fits on top of it.

• Slide the piston out of the siphon unit, remove any washers and springs fitted to it and slide off the old flap valve (D). Take it with you to your plumbing supplier so you can select a matching replacement.

• Fit the replacement flap valve on top of the piston and re-assemble everything in reverse order. Trim it to size first with scissors if it is a little larger than the old flap valve.

• Finally, restore the water supply and enjoy a one-touch flush again.

 C

 D

the home doctor

A: This is happening because the cistern is overfilling. This can happen if the float-operated arm of the ball valve is badly adjusted, allowing water to carry on dripping into the cistern between flushes until it eventually overflows.

• Lift off the cistern lid and flush the WC. Push the float arm down and adjust the small screw on it that presses against the valve body. Making it project more towards the valve body will close the valve earlier and stop the cistern overfilling.

• Let the cistern refill and check that the valve closes with the water level about 10 mm (⅜ in) below the overflow pipe. Make a further adjustment if necessary.

Q: There's a constant drip from the upstairs WC's overflow pipe, which is staining the house wall below. How can I fix it?

A: There's nothing more panic-inducing than a blocked loo. Be ready for it by keeping a large rubber-cupped plunger handy.

• Fit the cup of the plunger over the outlet at the base of the pan, and thrust it down and up and down again several times. This should clear a toilet paper blockage.

• When the pan has emptied, chuck a bucket of water down the pan to sluice the soil pipe through.

• If the blockage simply refuses to shift, call out a plumber as soon as you can.

Q: The WC gets blocked up now and then when the children use too much loo paper. What's the best unblocker?

windows 1

Your windows have a lot to put up with. They're opened and shut all the time, they're often left to blow about in the wind and they seem to attract children's footballs like magnets. Then there's the weather, alternately soaking and roasting them and causing all sorts of stresses and strains. Here's how to give yours some first aid.

Q: My windows are really hard to open and shut, and I'm afraid I'll crack the glass by forcing them. What should I do?

A: If your windows are hard to open, the wood has probably swollen after a period of damp or humid weather. It does this if moisture can get into the wood through defects in the paintwork, open joints in the window frame and even through parts that haven't been painted because they're out of sight, such as the top and bottom edges of the window.

Windows can also bind if they've been repainted regularly over the years. The paint thickness builds up to the point where the window simply won't close without a struggle. And a window that was closed too soon after repainting may simply be stuck fast.

• Run a knife blade all round the stuck window, both inside and out (A). Be careful not to cut into the woodwork.

• Release the window catches and try pushing the window open. Even if it won't budge, you might find that it's binding at just one corner. Hold a piece of scrap wood against the frame, close to the sticking corner, and give it a

A

B

C

couple of firm taps with your hammer to free it (B).

• Use a plane or Surform to shave the edge of the frame, cutting back to bare wood (C). Close and open the window to check
that it now works freely, removing a little more wood if it still seems to bind.

• Sand the edge smooth and apply a primer-undercoat or a first coat of microporous paint. (The advantage of using microporous paint instead of traditional gloss is that it allows damp wood to dry out, so your window shouldn't swell and bind any more. However, it works only on bare wood.) Leave the paint to dry for the recommended time, then apply a top coat. Paint the top and bottom of the window too, if they haven't been painted before.

A: Each sash has a weight at each side, and if one of the cords breaks the sash tends to jam in its tracks. It's time to take things apart. How much depends on whether it's the inner or outer sash that's affected, but while you're at it, you may as well replace all the cords – another is sure to break soon if you don't.

• Prise off the staff bead that retains the inner sash in its frame. You can then swing the inner sash into the room and cut the remaining cord close to its fixing nails. Lift the sash out and remove the remains of the cords from its edges.

• If the outer sash is affected, prise off the parting bead that separates the two sashes so you can lift out the outer sash. Then you will be able to cut and remove the cords.

• Prise out the pocket covers at each side of the frame so you can remove the weights and the rest of the old cords. Measure the total length of each cord and cut new pieces of sash cord to match.

• Attach a slim weight such as a nail to some thread and feed it over each pulley so the nail drops inside the weight compartment. Tie the nail end of the thread to the cord and use the thread to pull the cord up and over the pulley. Then tie one end of the cord to the weight. Repeat for the other three weights.

• Get a helper to support the outer sash while you nail the other ends of the cords to its sides. Fit the sash back in place in the frame and replace the parting bead.

• Repeat the process for the inner sash and replace the staff bead. Finally replace the pocket covers and check that the window now opens and closes smoothly.

Q: My sash windows won't stay open because one of the cords has broken and dissapeared into the weight componant. How do I go about fixing it?

SASH WINDOW PARTS

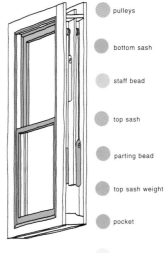

pulleys

bottom sash

staff bead

top sash

parting bead

top sash weight

pocket

bottom sash weight

windows 2

The most fragile part of any window is the glass. It can be broken by flying objects, and it can crack or shatter if the window slams after being left off its catch to swing freely in the wind. Breaking a window is also a favourite way for a burglar to get in, enabling him to reach the catch from outside.

Q: My kids have just broken the kitchen window with a football. How do I go about replacing it?

A: If a window is cracked – or, worse still, smashed to bits – you need to fix it fast to keep the weather out and your house secure. Fitting a new pane isn't difficult, but you'll need help if it's bigger than about 1000 mm (3 ft) across; you might prefer to call in a glazier to replace a large pane.

• If the damage occurs when local glass suppliers are closed, make a temporary repair by taping a polythene dust sheet or opened-out plastic shopping bags to the inside of the broken pane.

• If the window is simply cracked, criss-cross the glass on the inside with masking tape, put on your gloves and goggles, then push pieces out by striking the glass with the handle of your hammer. Once you've created a hole, wriggle the rest of the glass free from the putty (A). If the window is broken, clear up the debris first, then carefully lift out the pieces still attached to the frame and put them in a cardboard box. Break any pieces that are too big by tapping them sharply with your hammer, tape up the box and put it out for the dustmen.

A

B

C

• Chisel or scrape out all the old putty from the recess (called a rebate) in which the glass fits (B). Use pliers to pull out any glazing sprigs you find buried in the putty. Measure the height and width of the rebate and take 3 mm (⅛ in) off each measurement so that the pane isn't too tight a fit. Then head off to your local glass merchant for supplies.

• Scoop out some putty and knead it in your hands until warm and soft. Squeeze it out between your thumb and forefinger into a thin sausage shape and press it into the rebate all round the frame (C).

• Lift in the glass, resting the bottom edge in the putty, and press it into place round the edges, not in the centre, to squash the putty and make a watertight seal. Tap in glazing sprigs at about 300 mm (12 in) intervals all round. Then press more putty into place to cover the edge of the glass, and use a putty knife to finish it to a smooth

45-degree angle. Trim off the excess putty on the inside, and leave it to harden for about three weeks before painting over it.

A: These panes are usually held in place by short lengths of shaped wooden beading fixed in place on the inside of the rebate the glass sits in.

• Prise them out with a chisel and remove the pins. Then tap out the remains of the pane. Save a piece so you can take it to your glass merchant, enabling him to match the thickness and any pattern or colour it has.

• Make a cardboard template of the pane. Tape the card over the hole on the inside of the door, then draw round its edges from the outside. Cut it out and check its fit – you should have about 2 mm (just under ⅛ in) of clearance all round, so trim it further if necessary.

• Take the template and the glass sample to your glass merchant. He will cut the replacement for you.

• Replace the pane on a thin layer of bedding putty and pin the beadings back into place to complete the repair.

Q: I've got four irregularly shaped panes of glass in the upper part of my front door, and a would-be burglar has broken one to try to reach the latch inside (thankfully it was deadlocked, so he didn't get in). How can I get a matching replacement for the smashed pane?

SEE ALSO:
Doors – pages 130–1
Draughts – pages 132–3

worktops

The plastic laminate surfaces on your kitchen worktops have to put up with a lot of wear and tear – things being spilt on them, hot pans being stood on them, sharp knives being used without a cutting board, and so on. They're surprisingly resilient, though, and with a little care they'll last for years.

Q: A gap keeps opening up between the back edge of my worktops and the wall behind, and I'm afraid spillages will drip down into the cupboards beneath. What should I do?

A: It's a good idea to seal this gap, both to prevent anything spilt on the worktop from running into it, and also to stop grease and food particles collecting there. The product to use is a mastic labelled for use in kitchens and bathrooms.

• To ensure a neat, professional-looking finish, stick masking tape to the worktop and to the wall, about 3 mm (⅛ in) from the edges of the gap (A). Make sure it's well pressed down on both surfaces.

• Fit the tube of mastic into your cartridge gun and make an angled cut across the nozzle to produce a bead of mastic that will just fill the gap (B).

• Squeeze the trigger to start the mastic flowing, and pipe a bead along the gap, keeping the gun moving at a steady pace to avoid a lumpy toothpaste effect (C).

• Form the bead into a neat concave cross-section by drawing a moistened finger or the handle of a teaspoon along it. Wipe off any excess mastic on to some kitchen paper (D).

A

B

C

D

- Leave the mastic for about 30 minutes to form a skin. Then peel off the strips of masking tape to leave perfect straight edges (E).
- If the bead becomes discoloured over time, you can remove it using proprietary silicone mastic remover. Then simply repeat the process to apply a fresh bead.

E

A: As they're often made from a plastic resin, worktops aren't immune to damage from heat or sharp implements.
- First try polishing the scratches out with metal polish, which is a mild abrasive. Even if this doesn't remove the scratches, it will remove ingrained dirt from them so that they won't be so noticeable.
- Next, try sanding the scratches out with fine steel wool. Form it into a pad to get a good grip and then scour the scratched area firmly. So long as the scratches are only in the clear surface layer, you shouldn't damage the design.
- Tackle the burn with wet-and-dry abrasive paper, used wet. Depending on how deep the burn is, you might eat into the layer carrying the design, but a small bare patch will look less noticeable than the original burn.

Q: Over the years my worktops have collected an assortment of scratches and cigarette burns. Can I remove them?

your home
log book

Keeping your home running smoothly is a bit like checking
over the family car. If you carry out regular inspections and do any necessary
maintenance, you'll avoid those expensive breakdowns that can cost a fortune
to fix. Here are four checklists to help you give your home the regular services
it needs. There's one for use every six months – say, in spring and autumn –
and three others: once a year, once every two years and once every five years.

You'll also find a section where you can record all the vital statistics of your
house – such as the locations of its services and any extensions or alterations
made to them by you, the presence of cavity wall insulation, the carrying out
of professional damp-proofing, and so on. Not only is this information useful
for you to have in one easily accessible place, it will also be invaluable to any
future owner of the property.

Finally, you'll find some useful advice about employing professional experts
when a job is beyond your DIY skills, plus the addresses and contact numbers
of several trade organizations that can put you in touch with registered
contractors or provide you with technical information. I hope you find it helpful.

6 month check-up

If you have an external TV aerial or satellite dish, use binoculars to check it from ground level.

Look for	DIY?	Do I Need an Expert?	Date Sorted
Mast leaning	Tighten fixings	Aerial specialist	
Aerial off direction	Match neighbours'	Aerial specialist	
Cable flapping	Secure to wall	No	

AIRBRICKS

Airbricks provide essential ventilation to underfloor voids and must be kept clear.

Look for	DIY?	Do I Need an Expert?	Date Sorted
Leaves and cobwebs	Clear blockage	No	
Soil over airbricks	Remove soil	No	
Only a few airbricks	Fit more airbricks	Builder	

CISTERNS

WC cisterns won't flush properly if they don't fill properly or the flap valve leaks, and they'll overflow if they overfill.

Look for	DIY?	Do I Need an Expert?	Date Sorted
Not filling to mark inside	Adjust float arm	No	
Not flushing properly	Replace flap valve	No	
Overflow dripping	Replace washer or diaphragm in valve; adjust float arm	No	

FENCES

Fence posts can work loose in high winds, panel fixings can tear out of the wood, and rot can damage any part of the fence.

Look for	DIY?	Do I Need an Expert?	Date Sorted
Loose posts	Set in concrete	Builder	
Rotten posts	Replace posts	Builder	
Damaged rails	Use repair brackets	No	
Loose panels	Use fixing clips	No	
Rotting panels	Use preservative	No	

FLASHINGS

Flashings are metal or mortar strips that seal the join between roof slopes and walls or chimney stacks above them. Use binoculars to inspect them.

Look for	DIY?	Do I Need an Expert?	Date Sorted
Metal flashings lifted	Press down	Roofer	
Metal flashings torn	Use repair tape	Roofer	
Metal flashings loose	Wedge into place	Roofer	
Mortar flashings cracked	Replace flashings	Roofer	

GUTTERS

Gutters can get blocked with wind-blown debris, such as leaves, and moss dislodged from the roof by birds. Inspect gutters from a ladder set up at eaves level.

Look for	DIY?	Do I Need an Expert?	Date Sorted
Blocked gutters	Clear debris	No	
Blocked downpipe inlets	Clear debris	No	
Blocked downpipes	Dismantle to clear	Builder	
Leaky gutter joints	Seal with mastic	No	
	or replace rubber joints		

HEATING

One of the commonest causes of problems with central heating is the header tank in the loft running low or empty. Check it when the heating is on.

Look for	DIY?	Do I Need an Expert?	Date Sorted
Low water level	Add water via tank ball-valve	No	
Empty tank	Repair or replace ball-valve	No	

RADIATORS

If there's any corrosion going on inside your heating system, your radiators will collect the gas produced.

Look for	DIY?	Do I Need an Expert?	Date Sorted
Radiators cold at top	Bleed off gas	No	
Radiators cold at base	Remove and clean	Plumber	
Radiators cold	Check valves are open	No	
Radiators leaking	Replace and add corrosion inhibitor	Plumber	

12 month check-up

BOILERS

Unless you have your boiler serviced regularly, it can become noisy and inefficient in operation, and might even become dangerous.

Look for	DIY?	Do I Need an Expert?	Date Sorted
Noisy operation	Add descaler to header tank.	No	
	Lower pump speed	No	
	If no change	CORGI fitter	
Constant on-off operation	No	CORGI fitter	
Soot around flue	No	CORGI fitter	

ELECTRICS

If your wiring system is protected by a residual current device (RCD), you should check that it's working by pressing its TEST button. Doing so should trip the RCD off. Since this will cut the power to appliances with clocks, save yourself the chore of resetting them all by doing the test in spring or autumn when the clocks have to be changed anyway. Call in an electrician if the RCD doesn't trip off or can't be switched back on.

FLEXES AND PLUGS

Portable appliances are plugged in and unplugged regularly, which can cause wear to the flex and make terminal screws work loose, causing short circuits.

Look for	DIY?	Do I Need an Expert?	Date Sorted
Damaged flex sheath	Replace flex	No	
Flex sheath outside plug	Remake connections	No	
Loose connections	Remake connections	No	
Incorrect fuse	Fit fuse of correct	No	
	rating for appliance		

GULLIES

Gullies are underground traps that link waste pipes and rainwater downpipes to the drains. They can become blocked by debris.

Look for	DIY?	Do I Need an Expert?	Date Sorted
Gully overflowing	Clear out trap	No	
Grating blocked	Clear debris	No	
Grating missing	Replace grating	No	

PIPEWORK

Supply and waste pipes can develop pinhole leaks, and screwed or push-fit connections can work loose.

Look for	DIY?	Do I Need an Expert?	Date Sorted
Green marks on copper	Clean pipe and tighten or re-solder connection	No	
Damp marks on the ceiling	Cut out pinholed pipe and replace	Plumber	
Damp patches on floor	Tighten connection	No	
	Suspect leak in concrete	Plumber	

ROOFS

Tiles and slates can be dislodged by high winds, while felted roofs can become torn or blistered as time goes by. Inspect them using binoculars or from a ladder set up at eaves level.

Look for	DIY?	Do I Need an Expert?	Date Sorted
Dislodged tile/slate	Replace tile/slate	Roofer	
Loose ridge tile	Rebed tile in mortar	Roofer	
Missing tile/slate	Fit replacement	Roofer	
Damaged roofing felt	Patch with mastic	No	

SMOKE DETECTORS

If a smoke detector is to do its job, it must be maintained in good working order at all times. Replace the battery without fail every year – on your birthday, for example.

Look for	DIY?	Do I Need an Expert?	Date Sorted
Dust and cobwebs	Open and clean inside	No	
Low battery beep	Replace battery	No	
Missing battery	Replace battery	No	

STOPTAPS

Stoptaps and isolating valves control the flow of water through your plumbing system, and are useless if they don't work when you need them.

Look for	DIY?	Do I Need an Expert?	Date Sorted
Stoptap or isolating valve stiff	Oil spindle	No	
Stoptap or isolating valve stuck	Turn with adjustable spanner	No	
Stoptap body dripping	Tighten gland nut	No	
Stoptap or isolating valve broken	Replace tap/valve	Plumber	

2 year check-up

CHIMNEYS

If you have a fire, stove or boiler burning coal or wood, you should have your chimney swept at least every couple of years to prevent a build-up of soot within the flue and avoid any risk of a chimney fire. Call in a sweep who is a member of the National Association of Chimney Sweeps.

DAMP

Damp is the result of water getting in through the house structure due to some defect in its waterproofing.

Look for	DIY?	Do I Need an Expert?	Date Sorted
Damp ceilings	Find and fix roof faults	Roofer	
	Fix plumbing leak in loft	Plumber	
Damp walls	Seal around window and door frames	No	
Damp walls	Inject new DPC	Damp specialist	
Damp concrete floor	Brush on new DPM	Damp specialist	

EAVES

Woodwork around the eaves is very exposed and can develop rot and insect infestation. The eaves may also help to ventilate the loft space.

Look for	DIY?	Do I Need an Expert?	Date Sorted
Rotten woodwork	Replace parts	Roofer	
Insect attack	Spray insecticide	No	

INSULATION

Insulation in the loft keeps heat in the rooms below, while insulation on loft tanks and pipes stops them freezing in winter.

Look for	DIY?	Do I Need an Expert?	Date Sorted
Displaced loft insulation	Replace insulation	No	
Damp loft insulation	Discard, lay vapour barrier, replace	No	
Insulation in eaves	Pull back to allow loft ventilation	No	
Dislodged tank insulation	Replace insulation	No	
Missing pipe insulation	Fit pipe insulation	No	

OUTBUILDINGS

Garages, garden sheds and greenhouses get less attention than the house, but still require an occasional maintenance once-over.

Look for	DIY?	Do I Need an Expert?	Date Sorted
Damaged roofing felt	Patch damage *or* replace felt	No	
Leaking corrugated roof	Patch with repair tape	No	
	Replace sheeting	Roofer	
Rotten woodwork	Replace wood	No	
Cracked glass	Patch with tape/replace	No	

PAINTWORK

Unless you have plastic windows and doors, you will need to give your exterior paintwork regular inspection.

Look for	DIY?	Do I Need an Expert?	Date Sorted
Loss of surface gloss	Repaint	No	
Blisters and cracks	Strip and repaint	No	
Loose/missing putty	Replace putty	Glazier	
Rotten woodwork	Replace wood	Carpenter if extensive	

PATIOS, PATHS AND STEPS

Hard surfaces out doors need to be level and firm, with no loose slabs or potholes to trip the unwary.

Look for	DIY?	Do I Need an Expert?	Date Sorted
Loose slabs	Re-lay on mortar	No	
Uneven slabs	Re-lay on sand bed	No	
Uneven paving blocks	Re-lay on sand bed	No	
Crumbling concrete	Dig up and replace	Builder	

WINDOWS AND DOORS

Apart from keeping an eye on their decorative order, give windows and doors a check-up to see that they're working properly.

Look for	DIY?	Do I Need an Expert?	Date Sorted
Window/door stiff	Plane binding edge	No	
Hinges loose	Re-attach hinges	No	
Hinges damaged	Replace hinges	No	
Window fittings loose	Re-attach fittings	No	

5 year check-up

CHIMNEYS

Your chimney stacks are the most exposed part of the house structure, and can develop dangerous defects out of sight. Inspect them with binoculars.

Look for	DIY?	Do I Need an Expert?	Date Sorted
Cracked pot	Remove/cap flue *or* replace pot	Builder	
Leaning pot	Re-set and re-make mortar around pot	Builder	
Damaged pointing	Replace pointing	Builder	
Leaning stack	No	Builder	
Loose/missing flashings	Replace flashings	Builder *or* roofer	

DRAINS

Drains are like Goldilocks: when they're good they're very very good, and when they're bad they're horrid. They deserve a little attention now and then.

Look for	DIY?	Do I Need an Expert?	Date Sorted
Cracked manhole covers	Replace cover	No	
Debris in manholes	Remove/hose out	No	
Water in manholes	Rod drains	Drain clearer	
Tree roots in drains	Remove roots and replace drain pipe	Drain layer	

GARDEN WALLS

If you have masonry walls around your garden, it pays to check their condition in case a collapse is imminent. You wouldn't want your property to be the cause of any injuries, would you?

Look for	DIY?	Do I Need an Expert?	Date Sorted
Defective pointing	Replace pointing	No	
Loose bricks/stones	Re-bed in mortar	No	
Loose coping stones	Re-bed in mortar	No	
Vertical cracks	Point cracks and keep under observation	No	
Wall leaning	Demolish and re-build wall	Builder	

HOUSE WALLS

Inspect your house walls for any defects that could lead to damp penetration or frost damage in the long term. See also Subsidence below.

Look for	DIY?	Do I Need an Expert?	Date Sorted
Dirty brickwork	Use pressure spray	Masonry cleaner	
Defective pointing	Replace pointing	Builder	
Bricks with split faces	Replace bricks	Builder	
Loose rendering	Replace rendering	Builder	
Soil above damp course	Remove soil	No	
White patches on bricks	Apply damp seal	No	
Stains on walls	Remove rusty fixings	No	

ROOF STRUCTURE

Get into your loft with a powerful torch and give the whole roof structure a close inspection for signs of water penetration, movement, insect attack or condensation.

Look for	DIY?	Do I Need an Expert?	Date Sorted
Stains on rafters	No	Roofer	
Daylight visible	No	Roofer	
Sagging rafters	No	Surveyor	
Woodworm holes	No	Woodworm specialist	

STAIRS

Check that the stair structure is sound and that everything is in its correct place.

Look for	DIY?	Do I Need an Expert?	Date Sorted
Loose treads	Screw treads to risers	No	
	Use repair brackets	No	
Loose or damaged handrail	Repair/replace rail	Carpenter	
Loose wedges	Drive back in place	No	

SUBSIDENCE

Houses built on clay soils can suffer from subsidence or from its opposite, heave. Both can cause severe structural problems.

Look for	DIY?	Do I Need an Expert?	Date Sorted
Zigzag cracks in walls	No	Building surveyor	
Gaps around floor concrete	No	Building surveyor	
Windows/doors binding	No	Building surveyor	

your house record

Use the page opposite to draw floor plans and record the important features of your house, such as where to turn off the water, gas and electricity, which electrical circuits control which lights and power points, and where the drains run. Add any other useful information about the house, such as whether any professional improvement or remedial work has been done and, if so, whether it carries a guarantee. You can even keep a note of your own DIY activities, recording how much paint it took to decorate the lounge, or how many rolls of wallpaper you put up in the stairwell. Not only will you find this an invaluable record; a copy of it would be much appreciated by anyone buying your house in the future.

HOUSE CONTROLS

Mark the locations of the following controls on your plans.

- Outside stoptap
- Indoor stoptap
- Gate valves on pipes from cold water tank
- Isolating valves on pipes to water-using appliances
- Drain valves on plumbing and heating circuits
- Top-up controls for sealed hot water or heating systems
- Main gas on-off lever
- Isolating valves on gas branch pipes
- Main electricity on-off switch
- Isolating switches for individual appliances (e.g. the cooker)
- Central heating programmer

ELECTRICITY CIRCUITS

Make a note here of which circuits in your consumer unit or fuse box control which circuits in your house, and number the fuses clearly from left to right so that you know which is which. You might have some or all of the following circuits:

- Lighting circuit 1 (5 or 6 amp/A)
- Lighting circuit 2 (5 or 6A)
- Outdoor lighting circuit (5, 6 or 10A)
- Socket outlet circuit 1 (30 or 32A)
- Socket outlet circuit 2 (30 or 32A)
- Socket outlet circuit 3 (30 or 32A)
- Outdoor sockets (30 or 32A)
- Water (immersion) heater (16 or 20A)
- Cooker (usually 45A)
- Shower (usually 45A)
- Burglar alarm (5 or 6A)
- Smoke detectors (5 or 6A)
- Doorbells (5 or 6A)

PROFESSIONAL WORK

Make a note here of any professional work you've had done on your house, with names, addresses and contact numbers where relevant.

- Home extensions or other major alterations (architect, surveyor, builder, etc.)
- Kitchen refit
- Bathroom refit
- Bedroom refit
- Replacement windows and doors
- Conservatory
- Central heating
- Rewiring
- Drive or garden landscaping
- Damp-proofing
- Rot treatment
- Woodworm treatment
- Cavity wall insulation

drawing to scale

The graph paper background allows you to draw simple floor plans to a scale of, say, 1:100. They don't have to be 100 per cent accurate – just good enough for you to be able to record the information you want. You can add room dimensions, which will be a useful guide when buying new floor coverings, and you can also mark the positions and sizes of windows as a reminder about curtain sizes. Use the page any way you want…

getting
professional help

Getting someone in to do home improvement work is a game otherwise known as dodging the cowboys. Everyone seems to have a horror story of the builders from hell, the plumbers who flooded the house, or the kitchen fitters who went on holiday – permanently. So what can you do to find a good, honest, reliable, trustworthy workman who can tell the time and hates Heavy Metal FM? Here are some points to help you steer clear of the incompetent, the lazy and the downright dishonest, who give decent craftsmen a bad name, and to make sure you get the job in hand done properly.

1 Go by personal recommendation

Ask neighbours, friends and relatives if they have employed anyone with experience of the sort of work you want done. This will also give you the chance to inspect the work personally.

2 Scout around

If you see a job like the one you want done being carried out locally, don't be afraid to approach the householder and ask how things are going. Alternatively, make a note of the contractor's number from his sign or van outside the house and make direct contact.

3 Let your fingers do the walking

Yellow Pages list contractors under individual trades. Look for display ads giving a description of the type of work the firm specializes in and, if possible, a logo indicating membership of an appropriate trade organization. Always call the association concerned first to check whether the claimed membership is genuine. When you've made your pick of the pack, call your chosen few – contact at least three firms – and ask if they will put you in touch with some satisfied customers locally so that you can inspect their workmanship and get a personal reference before going ahead.

4 Ask for a quotation

Write to the contractors you have selected and ask them to give you a quotation (often abbreviated to 'quote' in the trade) for the work you want done. For a relatively simple job, they might be able to do this after a site visit. For more complicated jobs, they'll also need written details and possibly plans from you. A quote is a fixed price for the work; ask how long the quoted price will remain valid, and whether it includes VAT. Check that the VAT number quoted is valid by calling your local VAT office. Unregistered cheats use fake VAT numbers to make an extra profit.

5 Check it out

When you get the quotations in, don't just pick the cheapest. It might indicate that the contractor will use cheap materials and sub-contract the work to inexperienced and cheaper workers. Equally, an absurdly high quotation is contractor-speak for, 'No, thanks – I don't want this particular job unless you're prepared to pay me massively over the odds.'

For a complex job, the quotation should include a schedule – a breakdown of the individual stages involved and a listing of specific materials or products to be used. If you didn't specify individual items, the contractor will include the cost of them within what is known as a provisional sum, and will replace it in the final bill by the actual net cost. The schedule should also indicate what parts of the job (if any) will be sub-contracted.

6 Look for insurance

Make sure the contractor has both employer's liability and public liability insurance, to cover them for any damage to property and for any injuries caused to their employees and third parties. Ask for the work to be covered by an insurance-backed warranty, such as the Federation of Master Builders' MasterBond scheme, to protect you if the firm concerned goes bust before finishing the work.

7 Use a contract

For small-scale jobs, a simple letter from you accepting the quotation at the given price will act as a contract. It should specify start and finish dates, how you will pay for the work and whether you will withhold any part of the payment as a retainer against the cost of putting right any defects in the finished job.

For bigger jobs, a full-scale contract is essential. The simplest option is to use the Building Contract for Home Owners/Occupiers published by the Joint Contracts Tribunal (JCT). This is an independent body which has produced this contract to make life easier for you and your contractor. It's won full marks from the Plain English Campaign for its simplicity, and costs about £10. Either ask your builder to use it, or order one from the JCT (telephone 0121 722 8200, fax 0121 722 8201).

8 Change your mind in writing

If you want to change something while the job is under way, discuss it immediately with your contractor. When you've agreed on the changes, put them in writing so that there's no scope for disagreement later. Include any change in the price due to the variation from the original contract. And if any problems arise during the job, talk about them straight away so that there's no chance of a potentially expensive misunderstanding. You don't want to fall out with your contractor – at least, not until he's finished.

9 Keep an eye on the job

Don't hover while work is in progress; nothing annoys contractors more. Instead, check progress each night, and if you find anything amiss either phone the contractor straight away, or leave written instructions for him to read in the morning. On long-running projects, suggest a short weekly meeting to discuss progress and sort out any problems.

10 Pay up on time

Once work is finished and you're satisfied, pay up promptly. It's not fair to withhold payment (apart from any agreed retainer) for labour and materials the contractor has had to pay for up front, and it's one of the biggest causes of complaint by contractors about their customers. However, don't be conned by contractors asking for money 'up front' for materials: if they don't have monthly accounts with their suppliers, they're not worth employing. And never pay in cash, however big the incentive of a 'cash discount' might seem. You'll just be fuelling the black economy.

11 Be patient

Remember, whatever you have done it is likely to involve lots of dirt and dust. So be prepared. Have plenty of plastic sheeting to cover furniture, carpets, etc. The builders will walk around in heavy boots and, however careful they are, your home will still seem like a building site. But be patient. It will be worth it in the long run when you see the effects of the improvement round your home.

how to contact contractors

The following trade organizations will supply you with a list of their registered contractors working in your area. Just give them a call.

BUILDERS AND ROOFERS

FEDERATION OF MASTER BUILDERS

Gordon Fisher House

14–15 Great James Street

London WC1N 3DP

Tel: 020 7242 7583

NATIONAL FEDERATION OF BUILDERS

Construction House

56–64 Leonard Street

London EC2A 4JX

Tel: 020 7608 5150

NATIONAL REGISTER OF WARRANTED BUILDERS

Gordon Fisher House

14–15 Great James Street

London WC1N 3DP

Tel: 020 7404 4155

SCOTTISH BUILDING CONTRACTORS' ASSOCIATION

13 Woodside Crescent

Glasgow G3 7UP

Tel: 0141 332 7144

DAMP, WOODWORM & ROT SPECIALISTS

BRITISH WOOD PRESERVING AND DAMP-PROOFING ASSOCIATION

6 The Office Village

4 Romford Road

London E15 4EA

Tel: 020 8519 2588

ELECTRICIANS

ELECTRICAL CONTRACTORS ASSOCIATION

ESCA House

34 Palace Court

London W2 4HY

Tel: 020 7313 4800

ELECTRICAL CONTRACTORS ASSOCIATION OF SCOTLAND

Bush House

Bush Estate

Midlothian EH26 0SB

Tel: 0131 445 5577

NATIONAL INSPECTION COUNCIL FOR ELECTRICAL INSTALLATION CONTRACTING (NICEIC)

Vintage House

37 Albert Embankment

London SE1 7UJ

Tel: 020 7564 2323

PLUMBERS AND HEATING ENGINEERS

ASSOCIATION OF PLUMBING AND HEATING CONTRACTORS

14–15 Ensign House

Ensign Business Centre

Westwood Way

Coventry CV4 8JA

Tel: 01203 470626

COUNCIL FOR REGISTERED GAS INSTALLERS (CORGI)

1 Elmwood

Chineham Business Park

Crockford Lane

Basingstoke

Hampshire RG24 8WG

Tel: 01256 372200

HEATING AND VENTILATING CONTRACTORS ASSOCIATION (HVCA)

Esca House
34 Palace Court
London W2 4JG
Tel: 020 7313 4900

INSTITUTE OF PLUMBING

64 Station Lane
Hornchurch
Essex RM12 6NB
Tel: 01708 472791

SCOTTISH AND NORTHERN IRELAND PLUMBING EMPLOYERS' FEDERATION

2 Walker Street
Edinburgh EH3 7LB
Tel: 0131 225 2255

ROOFERS

CONFEDERATION OF ROOFING CONTRACTORS

72 Church Road
Brightlingsea
Colchester
Essex CO7 0JF
Tel: 01206 306600

NATIONAL FEDERATION OF ROOFING CONTRACTORS

24 Weymouth Street
London W1N 4LX
Tel: 020 7436 0387

CONVERSIONS

If you're happy working entirely in metric figures, good for you. They're generally easier (and therefore more accurate) to use than imperial measures, because they don't involve any potentially confusing fractions. If you still tend to think in imperial terms, here are some rough conversion factors to use for approximations only.

- 300 millimetres (mm) equal roughly 1 foot (ft)
- 900 mm is roughly 1 yard (yd)
- 500 millilitres (ml) is just less than 1 pint
- 4.5 litres is roughly 1 gallon
- 1 kilogram (kg) is just over 2 lb
- 50 kg is roughly 1 hundredweight (cwt)
- 1 square metre (sq m or m²) is about 11 square feet
- 1 cubic metre (cu m or m³) is about 1⅓ cubic yards

For precise conversions, use the following with a calculator.

1 in = 25.4 mm	**1 mm** = 0.0394 in
1 ft = 305 mm	**100 mm** = 3.94 in
1 yd = 915 mm	**1 metre** (m) = 39.37 in
1 sq ft = 0.0929 sq m	**1 sq m** = 10.764 sq ft
1 cu ft = 0.028 cu m	**1 cu m** = 1.308 cu yd
1 lb = 454 grams (g)	**1 kg** = 2.205 lb
1 ton = 1016 kg	**1 tonne** = 2205 lb
1 pint = 568 ml	**1 litre** = 1.76 pints
1 gallon = 4.546 litres	**5 litres** = 1.1 gallons

top tip

Dodging cowboys on the web

There are currently two free-access websites that can put you in touch with carefully vetted contractors and offer you a guarantee against the contractor going bankrupt. More are sure to follow. You can visit them at: www.hi-revolution.com and www.improveline.com

glossary

Here's a selection of technical terms that could help you make sense of contractors' quotations, and talk to them in their own language.

alkyd resins are used as binders in modern solvent-based paints in place of linseed oil, which gave oil paints their name.

Anaglypta is a trade name for a relief wall covering made from wood pulp. It's intended for overpainting once hung.

architraves are timber mouldings nailed to the edges of door frames to hide the join between the frame and the wall.

arris rails are the triangular horizontals fixed between fence posts to which the vertical boards are nailed to make up a boarded fence.

Artex is also a trade name, for a textured coating used on walls and ceilings. Original Artex was a powder that had to be mixed with water, but most textured coatings are now ready-mixed.

ball valves are float-operated valves fitted in storage and WC cisterns to refill them automatically after water has been drawn from them.

balusters are decorative vertical posts used beneath a handrail to make up a balustrade on stairs and around landings.

bargeboards are timber or plastic boards used to finish off the roof edge at gable ends.

casement windows have side-hung opening casements and top-hung vents, plus one or more fixed panes.

consumer unit is the control panel for your home's electricity supply, housing the main on-off switch and the various fuses or circuit breakers that protect individual circuits.

coving is a decorative moulding of plaster, plasterboard or foamed plastic used to conceal the join between walls and ceilings.

cross-lining means hanging plain lining paper horizontally on walls before hanging another wall covering over it vertically.

damp-proof course (DPC) is a waterproof layer built into house walls just above ground level to stop damp rising in the masonry. A damp-proof membrane (DPM) is included in solid concrete floors for the same reason.

drop-pattern wallpaper has a pattern that drops by half a repeat across the width.

eggshell paint is a solvent-based paint that dries to a matt finish rather than a high gloss.

fascias are vertical planks nailed to the cut ends of roof rafters at the eaves. Where the eaves overhang the wall below, a horizontal board called a 'soffit' fills the gap between fascia and wall.

flashings are strips of waterproof materials – usually metal or felt – used to waterproof the join between a roof and a higher wall.

flaunching is the technical term for the sloping mortar cap on a chimney stack that holds the pot in place.

gate valves are on-off valves fitted on low-pressure pipe runs so that you can turn off the water flow to whatever the pipe supplies.

grout is a powder or ready-mixed product used to fill the narrow gaps left after ceramic tiles have been stuck to walls or floors.

knotting is a sealer used to cover knots in woodwork, preventing resin from oozing out and spoiling the finish.

lath and plaster comprises thin pieces of wood (the laths) nailed across the underside of ceiling joists or the uprights of timber-framed walls and covered with plaster to form a hard ceiling or wall surface. Plasterboard is now used instead.

Lincrusta is a relief wall covering made from a mixture of linseed oil and fillers, hardened into rolls or panels.

lining paper is plain paper hung to provide a stable base for other wallcoverings. A special grade is available for overpainting.

lintels are beams spanning door or window openings, and support the wall above. They can be made of timber, stone, steel or reinforced concrete.

manholes or inspection chambers are brick or plastic underground pits installed on drain runs where branch drains join the main run, or where the drains change direction.

mastic is a non-setting sealant used to fill gaps between building components, such as door or window frames, and the masonry.

miniature circuit breakers (MCBs) are switches used instead of circuit fuses in a consumer unit to protect circuits in the house from overloading.

newel posts are the main vertical timbers in staircase construction, the handrail at each change of direction.

noggings are short horizontal timber braces fitted between the vertical posts (called studs) in a timber-framed partition wall.

primers are used on many surfaces to seal them and provide a sound base for subsequent coatings.

relief wall coverings are plain embossed papers designed to be overpainted once hung.

residual current devices (RCDs) are safety devices fitted to the house wiring to detect current leaks that could cause an electric shock or start a fire.

reveals are the vertical sides of a recessed door or window opening.

ring mains are electrical circuits supplying socket outlets, and are wired as a ring with both ends of the circuit cable connected to the same fuseway in the consumer unit.

rising main is the incoming mains-pressure water pipe. It enters the house from below ground and rises up to the storage cistern in the loft.

self-smoothing compound is a cement-based material used on concrete floors to provide a smooth, level surface before laying floor coverings.

solvent-based paints like gloss and eggshell are used mainly on wood and metal, and need white spirit as a thinner and cleaning agent.

spurs are cable branch lines connected to a house wiring circuit to supply extra lights or socket outlets.

stoptaps (also known as stopcocks) are fitted on the house's mains water supply pipe to allow the flow to be regulated or turned off completely.

strings are the two sloping members at each side of a staircase, supporting the treads and the risers (the verticals between the treads).

vinyl wall coverings have the design printed on a PVC layer, which is stuck to a paper backing. They can be stripped without wetting because the plastic layer simply peels off.

washable wallpapers are printed papers with a clear plastic coating for protection. You need a steam stripper to remove them.

woodchip paper is a wallcovering made by including chips of wood in the pulp. It needs painting once hung, and is a good cover-up for poor walls.

index

Page numbers in italics refer to illustrations

PICTURE CREDITS

BBC Worldwide would like to thank the following for providing photographs and for permission to reproduce copyright material. While every effort has been made to trace and acknowledge all copyright holders, we would like to apologise should there have been any errors or omissions.

Copyright BBC Worldwide (Ray Moller): cover. (J.Buckley): 33. (Paul Bricknell): 38, 50–7, 60, 63, 68r, 79r, 89–94, 102–5, 109, 137, 163. (Andy Woods): 40–9, 58, 66, 70–7, 80–1, 87, 95, 98–101, 106, 110–13, 117, 123, 125, 133, 152–3, 155, 164–5. (Tim Young): 120, 144–7, 150.

BBC Good Homes Magazine (Tim Young): 17. (Lucinda Symonds): 36. (Robin Matthews): 68–9, 79, 82–5, 97, 108, 114, 115b, 118, 130–2, 134–6, 139–143, 149, 154, 158–161, 166–7. (Shona Woods): 66.

Arcaid/David Churchill (10b); Richard Burbridge 157; DIY Photo Library 30, 31, 34, 64–5; Elizabeth Whiting Associates 8, 10t, 19, 35, 96, 128, 129, 172; Robert Harding 6bc, 11, 115, 127; MFI Home Works 32, 35t, 107; Narratives 2, 119.